Every Person's Guide to

JUDAISM

Stephen J. Einstein
and Lydia Kukoff

◆ ◆ ◆

UAHC Press

New York, New York

Cover: Detail of the Ten Commandments, Torah ark door;
Poland, early 18th century. From the collection
of the Hebrew Union College Skirball Museum,
photography by John R. Forsman.

Library of Congress Cataloging-in-Publication Data
Einstein, Stephen J.
  Every person's guide to Judaism / Stephen J. Einstein
and Lydia Kukoff.
    p. cm.
  Bibliography: p.
  Includes index.
  ISBN 0-8074-0434-9
  1. Judaism—Customs and practices.   2. Fasts and feasts—Judaism.
3. Judaism—20th century.   I. Kukoff, Lydia.   II. Title.
BM700.E339   1989
296—dc19   89–4719
                                                  CIP

We gratefully dedicate
this book to

Charles and Lynn Schusterman

who in the finest tradition of Judaism
did
so that generations yet to come might
hearken

נַעֲשֶׂה וְנִשְׁמָע   שמות כד־ז

[All that God has spoken] we will
do, and hearken

Exodus 24:7

I gratefully dedicate this book to my wife, Robin, and to our children, Rebecca, Jennifer, Heath, and Zachary. Their love and devotion have been both comfort and inspiration to me.

Stephen J. Einstein

I lovingly dedicate this book to my beloved husband and soul's companion, Ben, and to our beloved children, David and Naomi, who continue to bring many blessings into my world.

Lydia Kukoff

Acknowledgments

We wish to thank the following people:

Robin Einstein, she of the eagle eye, who typed the entire manuscript with careful attention to detail and challenged us to be as thorough as possible.

Rabbi Daniel B. Syme for his constant support and encouragement of this project.

Nancy Berman, director of the Hebrew Union College Skirball Museum, and her staff for graciously sharing the riches of the museum with the readers of this book.

Susanne Kester who helped us select the art, which so enriches the text. Her encyclopedic knowledge and love of the Judaica in the collection of the Hebrew Union College Skirball Museum both assisted and inspired us.

Mickey Finn who assisted in the preparation of this manuscript.

Annette Abramson who calmly, caringly, and tirelessly copy edited this manuscript.

And, finally, our readers:

Sherri Alper
Dr. Linda Chiou
Louise Driben
Deborah Chism Globerson
Dru Greenwood
Rabbi Daniel B. Syme
Dr. Donald J. Weinstock

whose helpful suggestions guided us in making the text clearer. We are grateful to them for taking the time to read the manuscript so carefully.

Contents

The Role of the Synagogue
Ashkenazic and Sephardic Customs
The Nature of the Community

Introduction

A story is told in the Talmud of a non-Jew who, in ancient times, came to the famous sage, Shammai, and asked him to explain the essence of Judaism while the questioner stood on one foot. Shammai, believing that the man was mocking him, sent him packing.

The man then approached Hillel, the other leading scholar of the age, with the very same question. Hillel accepted the challenge and gave this response: "What is hurtful to you, do not do to others. That is the whole Torah; the rest is commentary. Now, go and study!"

From this we learn that, while Judaism can be distilled into a basic ethical principle, that principle does not exhaust all of Judaism. Similarly, in this book we attempt to present a primer of Jewish life, recognizing that it is only the first step to future Jewish learning and living.

Jewish life is nearly endless in its variety. Because ours is an ancient culture and Jews have lived in so many places over the centuries, a tremendous number of differing customs have developed. In whatever country Jews have lived, Judaism—in custom as well as philosophy—has been influenced by the surrounding culture and has, in turn, been an influence on that culture. A major twentieth-century Jewish thinker, Mordecai M. Kaplan, has aptly described Judaism as an evolving religious civilization.

While Judaism is a religion, it is more than that. Judaism encompasses religion, history, language, culture—it is a civilization. Being Jewish is not only being part of a faith community, it is being part of a people.

There is a wide diversity of belief and practice within the Jewish community. It is our goal in this book to articulate that diversity by highlighting a variety of customs and exploring the philosophies that underlie them.

We have chosen to focus on the holidays and life-cycle events because they reveal so much about Judaism. However, this book is not simply about customs and ceremonies. Its focus is the deep connection between Jewish theology and Jewish living. Judaism is not merely a religion; it is a system that suffuses the life of its adherents.

No one book on Judaism can ever hope to express its infinite richness. This slim volume merely begins what we hope will be a lifelong pursuit for its readers. Now, go and study!

The Cycle of the Year

◆ ◆ ◆

THE JEWISH CALENDAR

THE SABBATH

HIGH HOLY DAYS

MAJOR FESTIVALS

MINOR FESTIVALS

NEW FESTIVALS

THE JEWISH CALENDAR

Jews often say: "The holidays are late this year" or "The holidays are early this year." In fact, the holidays never are early or late; they are always on time, according to the Jewish calendar.

Unlike the Gregorian (civil) calendar, which is based on the sun (solar), the Jewish calendar is based primarily on the moon (lunar), with periodic adjustments made to account for the differences between the solar and lunar cycles. Therefore, the Jewish calendar might be described as both solar and lunar. The moon takes an average of twenty-nine and one-half days to complete its cycle; twelve lunar months equal 354 days. A solar year is 365¼ days. There is a difference of eleven days per year. To ensure that the Jewish holidays always fall in the proper season, an extra month is added to the Hebrew calendar seven times out of every nineteen years. If this were not done, the fall harvest festival of *Sukot,* for instance, would sometimes be celebrated in the summer, or the spring holiday of *Pesach* would sometimes occur in the winter.

Jewish days are reckoned from sunset to sunset rather than from dawn or midnight. The basis for this is biblical. In the story of Creation (Genesis 1), each day concludes with the phrase: "And there was evening and there was morning. . . ." Since evening is mentioned first, the ancient rabbis concluded that in a day evening precedes morning.

· 3

The following list of the Hebrew months and the holidays that occur during these months also indicates the corresponding secular months.

Hebrew Months	Jewish Holidays	Secular Months
Nisan	Pesach, Yom Hashoah	March–April
Iyar	Yom Ha'atsmaut	April–May
Sivan	Shavuot	May–June
Tamuz		June–July
Av	Tishah Be'av	July–August
Elul		August–September
Tishri	Rosh Hashanah, Yom Kippur, Sukot, Simchat Torah	September–October
Cheshvan		October–November
Kislev	Chanukah	November–December
Tevet		December–January
Shevat	Tu Bishvat	January–February
Adar	Purim	February–March

For the counting of *months, Nisan*—the month that begins spring—is considered the first. However, the Jewish *year* is reckoned from the month of *Tishri*—the month that begins autumn. This would seem to be the superimposition of one calendar system upon another, which took place during the Babylonian Exile (sixth pre-Christian century).

According to Jewish tradition, history is reckoned from the time of Creation; Jewish years, therefore, are numbered from then. For instance, Israel declared its independence on 5 *Iyar* 5708 (corresponding to May 14, 1948). The year 5708 (and every Jewish year) was figured by commencing the count from the very beginning of Genesis.

Christian custom has been to divide history into two periods: before the time of Jesus (called B.C. = before Christ) and after Jesus' birth (called A.D. = *anno Domini* = in the year of the Lord). Jewish books generally refer to these periods as B.C.E. (before the common era) and C.E. (of the common era).

The subject of the calendar is rather complex. We have, therefore, touched only its broadest outlines. Since the rhythm of Jewish life is fixed by the calendar, we now turn to the times and seasons that make up the Jewish year.

THE SABBATH

· 1 ·

Building a Palace in Time: Shabbat

When most people think of holidays, they think of *annual* celebrations, but in Judaism there is one holiday that occurs every week—the Sabbath. Known in Hebrew as *Shabbat* and in Yiddish as *Shabbos,* this holiday is central to Jewish life. As the great Jewish writer Ahad Ha-Am has observed: "More than the Jewish people has kept the Sabbath, the Sabbath has kept the Jewish people." The Sabbath truly has been a unifying force for Jews the world over.

Shabbat is observed on the seventh day of the week in fulfillment of the biblical commandment: "Six days you shall labor and do all your work, but the seventh day is a sabbath of the Lord your God." (Exodus 20:9–10) In accordance with the Jewish calendar, the Sabbath begins on Friday evening at sunset and ends on Saturday night with the appearance of three stars. All Jewish days begin at sunset. This reckoning is based on the wording of the Creation story in Genesis 1. At the end of the description of each day, we find the phrase: "And there was evening, and there was morning. . . ." Since evening is mentioned first, the ancient rabbis deduced that evening *is* first.

Sanctification of Time

While *Shabbat* occurs on Friday evening and Saturday, it is more than simply another day in the week. It is a special day, and we invest it with specialness. Friday and Saturday come automatically, but *Shabbat* takes place only when we make it happen. We must make the decision to establish *Shabbat* in our own lives if we want to have it. In order to allow *Shabbat* to enter our lives, it is necessary to prepare ourselves and our environment. We prepare for *Shabbat* by the clothes we wear, by the meals we eat, by the lighting of Sabbath candles, and by chanting the *Kiddush* over wine to set apart this special time.

Shabbat is such a special time that it has been likened to the Messianic Age. A well-known *midrash* expresses this thought:

> When God was about to give the Torah to the Jewish people, God summoned the people and said to them: "My children, I have something precious that I would like to give you for all time, if you will accept My Torah and observe My commandments."
>
> The people then asked: "Ruler of the universe, what is that precious gift You have for us?"
>
> The Holy One, blessed be God, replied: "It is the world-to-come (the Messianic Age)!"
>
> The people of Israel answered: "Show us a sample of the world-to-come."
>
> The Holy One, blessed be God, said: "The *Shabbat* is a sample of the world-to-come, for that world will be one long *Shabbat*."

Concept of the Messiah

This is an appropriate time for us to talk about the Jewish view of the Messiah. The word "messiah" is derived from the Hebrew word *mashiach,* which literally means "anointed one." In the days of the Bible, anointing a person with oil was a way of declaring him king. Thus, messiah means king—a flesh-and-blood king, *not* a divine being.

Messianic expectations developed over time. In the fully developed form of this idea, the Messiah would (1) establish himself as the king, (2) gain independence for the Jewish people in their own land, (3) be an ideal king, and (4) with God's help, establish peace, justice, and brotherhood—not only for the Jews, but for all the world.

Throughout Jewish history, there were a number of individuals who claimed to be the Messiah. While each of these people gained some following at first, *none* of them—*including Jesus*—fulfilled the messianic expectations. Thus, in Judaism, no one has been accepted as the Messiah.

The early Church realized that Jesus did not do all that was expected of the Messiah. It insisted that he would return to earth someday to complete the task. This doctrine is known as the "Second Coming of Christ." Judaism has maintained that, as long as messianic expectations remain unfulfilled, the Messianic Age is still a hope for the future.

Incidentally, knowledgeable Jews don't refer to Jesus as "Christ" since "Christ" is a title meaning "anointed one," and Jews do not believe that Jesus was the Anointed One. Though Jesus has no role whatsoever in Judaism, most Jews would say that he was a fine teacher whose teachings have had a considerable influence on the world. A good deal of what he taught was basic Judaism.

In rabbinic literature, there was some speculation about personal characteristics of the Messiah. However, great importance was placed on what would be the results of the coming of the Messiah—the Messianic Age. Reform and Conservative Jews generally emphasize the Messianic Age rather than a personal Messiah. The Messianic Age can be compared to a jigsaw puzzle. Each individual has a piece of the Messiah within. We have to put all our pieces together if we want to build a better world.

Creation and Re-creation

Shabbat is a day of rest. However, it's not just a day to sleep late. The paradigm for Sabbath rest can be found in Genesis 2:1–3: "The heaven and the earth were finished, and all their array. On the seventh day God finished the work which He had been doing, and He ceased [rested] on the seventh day from all the work which He had done. And God blessed the seventh day and declared it holy, because on it God ceased [rested] from all the work of creation which He had done." Thus the pattern of work and rest is woven into the very fabric of the universe. Rest means more than physical cessation of work. It implies taking oneself out of the ordinary, out of the routine, out of the rat race. This kind of rest gives us the opportunity to re-create our spirit and restore our soul. *Shabbat* is a time that is set aside to take notice of the wonders around us.

This thought is echoed in a Sabbath eve reading in *Gates of Prayer,* the prayer book of the Reform movement:

There are days
when we seek things for ourselves and measure
failure by
what we do not gain.

On the Sabbath
we seek not to acquire but to share.

There are days
when we exploit nature as if it were a horn
of plenty that can
never be exhausted.

On the Sabbath
we stand in wonder before the mystery of
creation.

There are days
when we act as if we cared nothing for the
rights of others.

On the Sabbath
we are reminded that justice is our duty and
a better world
our goal.

> (*Gates of Prayer,* pp. 177–178)

Not only is the Sabbath an integral part of the Creation story, it is the only holiday mentioned in the Ten Commandments. The Ten Commandments actually appear twice in the Bible. The Sabbath commandment is formulated somewhat differently in each instance.

Remember the sabbath day and keep it holy. Six days you shall labor and do all your work, but the seventh day is a sabbath of the Lord your God: you shall not do any work—you, your son or daughter, your male or female slave, or your cattle, or the stranger who is within your settlements. For in six days the Lord made heaven and earth and sea, and all that is in them, and He rested on the seventh day; therefore the Lord blessed the sabbath day and hallowed it.

(Exodus 20:8–11)

Observe the sabbath day and keep it holy, as the Lord your God has commanded you. Six days you shall labor and do all your work, but the seventh day is a sabbath of the Lord your God: you shall not do any work—you, your son or your daughter, your male or female slave, your ox or your ass, or any of your cattle, or the stranger in your settlements, so that your male and female slave may rest as you do. Remember that you were a slave in the land of Egypt and the Lord your God freed you from there with a mighty hand and an outstretched arm; therefore the Lord your God has commanded you to observe the sabbath day.

(Deuteronomy 5:12–15)

These passages, while essentially the same, point out two different aspects of *Shabbat*. Exodus tells us to remember the Sabbath while Deuteronomy stresses the observance of the day. Furthermore, each passage gives a different rationale for *Shabbat*. Exodus reminds us that on *Shabbat* we rejoice in the creation of the physical universe. Deuteronomy points out that we must remember the Exodus from Egypt. In so doing, we are cognizant of the freedom we enjoy.

Covenant and Chosenness

Shabbat is also seen as a sign of a covenant between God and the Jewish people. The Hebrew words of Exodus 31:16–17, sung at *Shabbat* services, emphasize the convenantal relationship: "The Israelite people shall keep the sabbath, observing the sabbath throughout the ages as a covenant for all time: it shall be a sign for all time between Me and the people of Israel. For in six days the Lord made heaven and earth, and on the seventh day He ceased from work and was refreshed."

Classic Jewish theology from the Bible onward has maintained that a special relationship exists between God and the Jewish people. This idea, referred to as the Chosen People concept, is one of the most misunderstood concepts within Judaism. Chosenness does *not* mean that Judaism teaches that Jews are better than everybody else in the world; it does *not* mean that Jews are elected for salvation. Judaism does not deny that God's love extends to all humanity. In fact, it affirms God's universal love in these words from the Midrash: "I call heaven and earth to witness: Gentile or Jew, man or woman, manservant or maidservant—all according to our deeds does the spirit of God rest upon us."

What, then, does chosenness imply? The traditional understanding is that God chose to establish a particular relationship with a certain individual, Abraham, and his descendants. The covenant, or agreement, between God and the Jewish people was that they—God and the Jewish people—would be loyal to one another.

The Torah says that, when God gave the commandments to the people of Israel, the people responded: "All that the Lord has spoken we will do and we will hear." (Exodus 24:7) Jews have never been satisfied to take the biblical text at face value but have always delved deeply into all of its ramifications.

The result of this process of delving is called *midrash*. For instance, when reading about the Israelites accepting the commandments so readily, our ancient rabbis wondered: "How might this have happened?" Two of the answers they came up with shed light on the concept of chosenness.

According to one interpretation, the Israelites were not God's first choice to receive the Torah. In fact, God had offered it to many other nations, but each of them had refused it. Only the Israelites were willing to say: "All that the Lord has spoken we will do and we will hear"; only they would accept the obligations of the covenant. In other words, the Jews were chosen, but they were not the first choice.

The second interpretation presents a much different view. In this *midrash*, the Israelites weren't all that willing to accept the Torah. Only when God threatened to drop Mount Sinai on them if they refused the Torah did they respond: "All that the Lord has spoken we will do and we will hear." In this version, the people may have felt that they were not adequate to the task, but they were compelled to rise to the challenge.

Very frankly, even after considering these interpretations of chosenness, some Jews are still not completely comfortable with the notion. So they interpret the concept more broadly. Rather than speaking in terms of God choosing the Jews, they understand chosenness to mean that the Jews chose God and the way of Torah.

For some Jews, even this interpretation is not acceptable. The Reconstructionist movement, for instance, rejects the notion of chosenness entirely and has changed those prayers that refer to chosenness.

Creating Shabbat in the Home

Much of our discussion up to this point has focused on concepts relating to *Shabbat*, but *Shabbat* truly becomes what it was meant to be as we bring it into our lives. We begin to create a *Shabbat* atmosphere by doing things in our home. We prepare the house for *Shabbat* by cleaning it and putting it in order. This may seem like a monumental task sometimes, but there are ways to get it done. For instance, this task can be shared or accomplished over several evenings. Playing Jewish music while you clean can help create the *Shabbat* mood, and you can learn a lot of Jewish songs in the process. Bringing in some fresh flowers makes the house more *Shabbosdik* (having a Sabbath atmosphere).

Friday night is a time for a special meal. This does not mean that the meal has to be expensive and elaborate. It should be special because of the love and care taken in its preparation and presentation. There are some foods that are traditional for *Shabbat*. Jews of Eastern European (Ashkenazic) background generally eat gefilte fish or chopped liver, chicken soup with *matzah* balls or noodles, roast chicken or brisket of beef, noodle or potato *kugel,* and *chalah.* Jews of Mediterranean (Sephardic) background eat foods that differ markedly. Some *Shabbat* favorites include fish with egg and lemon sauce, eggplant salad, lamb roast, stuffed grape leaves, and white rice.

While these are traditional foods, you should not feel restricted to these. You can experiment or use your own favorites.

The table should be set as befits a visit by a queen since *Shabbat* is metaphorically seen as a queen. Place on the table an attractive cloth or place mats and your finest dishes and flatware. Also, on the table (or on a nearby table) should be placed candlesticks and candles, a *Kiddush* cup and wine, one or two *chalot* covered with a *chalah* cover or napkin, and salt.

Shabbat is welcomed by a ceremony at the table prior to the meal. While the ceremony formally begins with the lighting of *Shabbat* candles, many people follow the custom of dropping some coins into a *pushke* (*tsedakah* box) first. While *tsedakah* is often translated as "charity," it doesn't really mean charity. The word is based on a Hebrew root meaning "righteousness" or "justice." The *mitzvah* (a religious obligation, which flows from the covenantal relationship between the Jewish people and God) of *tsedakah* places on every Jew the obligation to right the injustices of society. One of the ways we do this is by contributing money to help individuals or groups who are in need themselves or who are engaged in helping others. While this may sound just like charity, it differs radically. There is no Hebrew word corresponding to what is expressed by the English word "charity." The crucial difference is in the attitude with which *tsedakah* is given. It is not seen as an act by

Chalah cover; Germany, 19th century. From the collection of the Hebrew Union College Skirball Museum, photography by John R. Forsman.

which one who is superior gives to one who is inferior. Nor is it something done out of love, as charity is. Rather, in order for us to be fully human, it is *incumbent* upon us to give and to give in such a way as to preserve the dignity of the recipient. Moses Maimonides, a great medieval philosopher, likened the giving of *tsedakah* to the rungs of a ladder. The lowest rung is giving grudgingly. A higher rung is to give anonymously. The very highest rung is to give in such a way as to enable the recipient to become independent.

There is a system of Hebrew numerology called *gematria* in which every Hebrew letter has a numerical equivalent. The Hebrew word for life, *chai*, consists of letters equaling 18 (*chet* = 8 and *yod* = 10). Therefore, *tsedakah* is often given in multiples of eighteen ($18, $36, $180, $360, etc.). By giving *tsedakah,* our goal is to enhance the lives of others.

It is customary to light at least two candles to welcome the Sabbath. One explanation for this is that each candle reminds us of one of the ways we are enjoined to celebrate the Sabbath ("Remember" and "Observe"). Some people light additional candles to represent the children in their family; others light one additional candle for each child in the family. The majority, however, simply light two candles. It is traditional for the woman of the house to light these candles and recite the blessing over them. If there is no woman, then the man lights the candles. In some families, the candle blessing is recited by the entire family.

There are various customs associated with the actual lighting of the candles. Some women, after kindling the candles, encircle the flames with their hands as a way of spreading the *Shabbat* light and drawing it close to themselves. You will also see some women cover their eyes with their hands after they have encircled the flames, while they say the blessing. The reason for this is actually a legal fiction. Normally, we recite a blessing before performing the act (such as reciting the blessing for bread before eating the bread). However, the procedure must be reversed when lighting the *Shabbat* candles. The candles must be lit first since, once the blessing has been said, *Shabbat* has begun and traditionally no fire can be created on *Shabbat*. By covering her eyes and not looking at the candles, it is as if the woman has not yet lit them. After completing the blessing, she removes her hands and looks at the candles as if for the first time. Everyone present then wishes each other *"Shabbat Shalom"* or *"Gut Shabbos."*

If you are not comfortable lighting the candles in either of these ways, it is perfectly acceptable to light them without placing your hands in front of your eyes. Some women choose to cover their eyes simply because it is a custom even though the rationale behind it is not particularly compelling for them. In many homes, a special set of candlesticks is set aside for Sabbath use. These may be silver, brass, wood, or ceramic. However, in the absence of specially designated candlesticks, you may use any candlesticks.

Scripture teaches that wine gladdens the human heart. We use wine for every special occasion. Each Sabbath and festival is welcomed and sanctified with a blessing over wine. Traditionally, kosher grape wine is used, but in some homes non-kosher wine is used. The wine for *Kiddush* is usually poured into a special *Kiddush* cup, which can be ceramic, glass, pewter, silver, etc. In the absence of a special *Kiddush* cup, any glass or goblet may be used.

The blessing over wine is called *Kiddush*. It is traditionally recited

Kiddush cups; Nürnberg (Nuremberg), Germany, early 18th century. From the collection of the Hebrew Union College Skirball Museum.

or chanted by the man of the house or by a guest. If there is no man present, a woman should say the *Kiddush*. In some homes, the entire family chants the *Kiddush* together. In addition to blessing God as the Creator of the fruit of the vine, the *Kiddush* also thanks God for the holiness of *Shabbat*. It states that *Shabbat* is a reminder of both Creation and the Exodus. As we say the *Kiddush* we think of the Creation story and the Garden of Eden, a paradigm of the perfect time that was. We think, too, of the Exodus, the time that signaled our redemption from servitude. Even as we look back to these events, we look forward to a time that will combine redemption and paradise—the Messianic Age. Before we drink the wine, we wish each other *"Lechayim"* (to life).

During the *Kiddush,* the *chalah* is covered with a decorated *chalah* cover or, in its absence, with a napkin. There is a reason often cited for this custom: At meals during the week, the blessing before eating is recited over bread. On *Shabbat,* before the blessing over bread, a much longer blessing—the *Kiddush*—is recited over wine. Unwilling to hurt the feelings of the bread by focusing all this attention on the wine, we cover the bread to avoid embarrassing it.

At first, this explanation may seem fanciful or even fatuous, but in fact it teaches a lesson in human relations. If we are called upon to concern ourselves with the feelings of a loaf of bread, how much more must we care about the feelings of our fellow human beings and be cognizant of how our words and actions affect them.

Chalah—a twisted egg bread, sometimes covered with sesame or poppy seeds—is the bread that is used for *Shabbat.* In Eastern Europe, weekday bread was very coarse while *chalah*—the *Shabbat* bread—was light and fine, made from more expensive flour. Some people set two *chalot* on the table as a reminder of the double portion of manna gathered by the Israelites on the day before the Sabbath. The Bible tells us that, during the wandering in the wilderness after the Exodus, God provided for all the physical needs of the Israelites. God provided a food called manna, which the people gathered daily. Since work was prohibited on *Shabbat,* and gathering manna would be considered work, God provided a double portion of manna on the day before the Sabbath to last them through *Shabbat.*

The blessing over bread, called the *Motzi,* thanks God "who brings forth (*hamotzi*) bread from the earth." Some people sprinkle the *chalah* with salt after making the blessing and before eating the bread. One explanation for this is that in Roman times salt was a very valuable commodity, available only to free people. By eating salt on *Shabbat,* we emphasize that we are free people serving God. Another explanation is that, since the destruction of the Temple in the year 70, the home has become "a small sanctuary" and the table an altar. Since the sacrifices were offered with salt, having salt on the table links us to our past. The home as sanctuary and the table as altar are underscored further by the tradition of speaking words of Torah at the table. In a Jewish home, mealtime should be more than a time for simply meeting one's physical needs; it should be a time for spiritual nourishment as well. A well-known talmudic statement teaches that, if three people sit at a meal and exchange words of Torah, it is as if the Divine Presence dwelt among them.

The Jewish blessing before a meal is a very brief one. A lengthier blessing is reserved for after the meal. This follows the biblical statement: "When you have eaten your fill, give thanks to the Lord your God. . . ." (Deuteronomy 8:10) There are several passages inserted into the blessing after the meal (*Birkat Hamazon*) that are only said on *Shabbat*. One of these prays for the coming of the time that will be entirely like *Shabbat*—the Messianic Age. Once again on this day of peace our thoughts are turned to the hoped-for redemption of the future.

Shabbat has another important element. It is a time of togetherness and joining—a time to be with friends and with family, taking time to appreciate each other. It is a nice custom to invite guests for *Shabbat*. Many people offer a word of appreciation to members of the family and friends at the Sabbath table. This might take the form of a husband reading Proverbs 31 to his wife and a parental blessing to the children. *Shabbat* is a time of union and harmony. Some Jews read verses from Song of Songs (a collection of beautiful love poems found in the Bible) on *Shabbat*. It is considered a *mitzvah* to make love on *Shabbat*, and it is said that God is present when husband and wife make love.

Celebrating Shabbat in the Synagogue

Another very important aspect of *Shabbat* is community. The community gathers for worship each *Shabbat*, reaffirming our covenantal tie to God and to one another. Some synagogues have their major Sabbath service on Friday evening while others have it on Saturday morning. The service consists of prayers and readings in Hebrew and English (the amount of Hebrew and English varies from synagogue to synagogue), songs, a Torah reading, and a talk. In many temples, after *Shabbat* evening services there is an *Oneg Shabbat* (joy of the Sabbath) at which refreshments are served and there is an opportunity to socialize. Sometimes Israeli dancing or a discussion takes place during the *Oneg*. Following *Shabbat* morning services, there is a *Kiddush* in the synagogue. After the blessings over the wine and the bread, people exchange *Shabbat* greetings.

One of the things that makes this day so special is that we eat so well. Many people have a large meal following the morning service and another smaller meal (*seudah shelishit*) before sunset.

Just as there is a ceremony welcoming *Shabbat*, so there is one to mark its conclusion. It is called *Havdalah*, which means "separation." The ceremony takes place on Saturday night after sunset. It consists

Spice box; Eastern Europe, 19th century. From the collection of the Hebrew Union College Skirball Museum.

of blessings over wine, spices, and a braided candle. While it resembles the Friday night ceremony in many ways, there are some differences as well. Wine is used at both ceremonies. Two candles and a braided *chalah* are used on Friday night while, on Saturday night, one braided candle with many wicks is used. The new element in the ceremony is the blessing of sweet-smelling spices. There is an explanation offered for this ceremony. Because *Shabbat* is such a special day, each Jew receives an extra soul at the beginning of the Sabbath, which departs at the end of *Shabbat*. To revive us, because we've lost this extra soul, we smell spices at *Havdalah,* bringing some of the sweetness of the Sabbath with us into the week. The climax of the ritual is when the candle is doused in the wine, and we stand in the darkness of the new week. But the darkness is not one of hopelessness; it is a time when we confront the new week with a vision of what we must do to bring about a better world. We sing the song of the prophet Elijah, symbol of the messianic future.

Study as a Form of Worship

Rest and worship are two essential elements of *Shabbat*. There is a third one that is of equal importance—study. *Shabbat* affords us time in which to direct our energies toward spiritual matters. Study is an appropriate way to observe *Shabbat*. In fact, in Judaism study is considered a form of worship. Study is done publicly at services by means of the Torah reading and its explanation, and privately by reading and discussing materials from Jewish books, magazines, and newspapers with family and friends.

Upon being exposed to the concepts and ideals of *Shabbat* for the first time, a student in one of our Introduction to Judaism classes wrote: "*Shabbat,* like Judaism, is a cornucopia of delight and joy for those who are willing to make the effort to find them; individual paths are different but they lead eventually, for those who pursue them, to an eminently worthwhile end: a foretaste of the Messianic Age."

The principle of *Shabbat* is to sanctify time. The whole of *Shabbat* is greater than the sum of its parts. It is more than lighting candles, drinking wine, or attending a service. We sanctify *Shabbat* by setting it apart, making it distinctive, and differentiating it from the rest of the days in our week. As Abraham Joshua Heschel has written: "Six days a week we live under the tyranny of things of space; on the Sabbath we try to become attuned to holiness in time."

(Abraham J. Heschel, *The Sabbath,* p. 8)

"Sabbath Afternoon," M. Oppenheim; Germany, 19th century. From the collection of the Hebrew Union College Skirball Museum, photography by Marvin Rand.

HIGH HOLY DAYS

·2·

Renewal: Rosh Hashanah

The Jewish year begins with the holiday called *Rosh Hashanah* (literally, the head of the year). It falls on the first day of the autumn month of *Tishri* and is celebrated for one day by most Reform Jews and for two days by Orthodox and Conservative Jews. It begins a ten-day period of intensive introspection known as *Yamim Noraim* (the Days of Awe), culminating with *Yom Kippur* (the Day of Atonement), a day of fasting. *Rosh Hashanah* and *Yom Kippur* together are called the High Holy Days, the High Holidays, or, more colloquially, the Holidays.

Rosh Hashanah marks, not only the beginning of a new year, but also, according to Jewish tradition, the celebration of the anniversary of the creation of the universe—the birthday of the world. In the words of a *Rosh Hashanah* prayer: "This day the world was called into being." Judaism teaches that creation is an ongoing process. As we read in our daily liturgy: "Every day God renews the work of creation." This process of re-creation takes place, not only in nature, but in the human soul as well. The High Holy Day season affords us the opportunity to reflect on the year just ending and to assess the direction of our lives for the year just beginning.

Preparation for the High Holy Days

Reflection requires preparation. It is unrealistic to expect that, merely by walking into the synagogue on *Rosh Hashanah* eve, one can easily

Shofar; Europe, 18th–19th century. From the collection of the Hebrew Union College Skirball Museum, photography by John R. Forsman.

enter into the rhythm of the season. For this reason, Jewish tradition prescribes a way to prepare ourselves spiritually for the High Holy Days, which includes the sounding of the *shofar* and the *Selichot* prayers.

For Jews, the *shofar* (ram's horn) is the symbol of the season, and the sound of the *shofar* evokes the mood and the spirit of *Rosh Hashanah*. The *shofar* is blown at weekday morning services during *Elul*, the month immediately preceding the High Holy Days, to remind the worshipers to begin the process of preparation.

Selichot are the penitential prayers traditionally recited in the very early morning prior to, and during, the High Holy Day season. Many synagogues hold *Selichot* services at midnight on the Saturday before *Rosh Hashanah*. (In order for the *Selichot* service to be truly preparatory, there needs to be ample time between *Selichot* and *Rosh Hashanah*. Therefore, if *Rosh Hashanah* falls on a Monday or Tuesday, *Selichot* services will be held at midnight on the Saturday of the preceding week.)

The High Holy Days exert a magnetic force, drawing Jews back to the synagogue. In order to accommodate the large number of worshipers, most synagogues issue tickets for seating. These tickets are generally included as part of temple membership, but nonmembers may purchase tickets on a space-available basis.

Another is to send greeting cards to friends and family. These are called *shanah tovah* (good year) cards. The greeting that is often printed on them is *Leshanah Tovah Tikatevu* (May you be inscribed for a good year). Sometimes this is shortened to *Shanah Tovah*. It is customary for Jews to greet one another at this time of the year using these same words. This greeting has its origin in the following legend:

> Rabbi Kruspedai said in the name of Rabbi Yochanan: "Three books are opened on *Rosh Hashanah,* one for the completely wicked, one for the completely righteous, and one for those in between. The completely righteous are immediately inscribed and sealed for life; the completely wicked are immediately inscribed and sealed for death; the fate of all others remains suspended from *Rosh Hashanah* until *Yom Kippur.* If they are found deserving, they are inscribed for life; if not, they are inscribed for death."   (*Mishnah Rosh Hashanah* 16b)

Since the final sealing of the decree, according to this passage, does not take place until *Yom Kippur,* it is customary to greet fellow Jews with the wish, *Gemar Chatimah Tovah* (May the final sealing be good), from the end of *Rosh Hashanah* through *Yom Kippur.*

Judgment

In our literature, the holiday of *Rosh Hashanah* is called by several names. One of these is *Yom Hadin* (the Day of Judgment). As the passage quoted above shows, the idea of being judged on this day goes back to talmudic times. (The Talmud was completed around the year 500.) Some Jews interpret this rather literally, asserting that God reviews their actions of the past year and judges them accordingly. Other Jews understand the judgment of this day as a process that occurs primarily within one's own conscience. As a matter of fact, the Hebrew word meaning "to pray" is *lehitpalel,* literally, to judge *oneself.*

Sin and Repentance

When most people think of judgment, they also think of sin. One of the Hebrew words for sin is *chet.* This was originally an archery term meaning "missing the mark." In using this word, Jewish tradition draws an analogy between life and archery. Just as an archer does not always hit the bull's-eye, so each of us does not always act in ways consonant with our own highest values. We sometimes "miss the mark."

Does this mean that Judaism says that every person is a sinner? While no one is perfect—everyone commits some wrongs—this is not the same as saying that it is our nature to be sinners. Original Sin is not a tenet of Judaism. Rather, Jewish tradition teaches that there dwells within each person both a good and an evil inclination. We are created with the capacity to choose between right and wrong, and it is *our* choice to make.

Why is "our" emphasized? Because the choice is not made by anyone other than ourselves. We are not "saved" by an outside agent. As a matter of fact, since there is no concept of Original Sin, we are not automatically doomed and need not be "saved" at all.

Although we are not sinners by nature, we sometimes feel as though we have missed the mark. How do we get back on target? The process of correcting one's course is called *teshuvah* (turning or returning, as in turning from an improper course to the proper course and returning to God).

Moses Maimonides, a great medieval Jewish philosopher, expressed the classic view on *teshuvah*. He wrote that *teshuvah* occurs when individuals recognize that they have erred, choose to correct their behavior, and vow not to repeat it. One knows that this process has been successfully accomplished when, faced with similar circumstances, one refrains from repeating the error.

The process of *teshuvah* begins with an intense examination of one's conscience. The high point of the *Rosh Hashanah* service is the blowing of the *shofar,* which is a call to conscience. When Jews hear the *shofar,* their souls are awakened to the possibilities of *teshuvah* and spiritual renewal.

The High Holy Days are a time for hearing—for really listening to the voices of those around us and to our own inner voice. This concept has been expressed beautifully by Rabbis Harold Kushner and Jack Riemer:

> Judaism begins with the commandment:
> Hear, O Israel!
> But what does it really mean to "hear"?

The person who attends a concert
While thinking of other matters,
Hears—but does not really hear.

The person who walks amid the songs of birds
Thinking only of what will be served for dinner,
Hears—but does not really hear.

The person who listens to the words of a friend,
Or mate, or child,
And does not catch the note of urgency:
"Notice me, help me, care about me,"
Hears—but does not really hear.

The person who stifles the sound of conscience
Saying, "I have done enough already,"
Hears—but does not really hear.

The person who listens to the rabbi's sermon
And thinks that someone else is being addressed,
Hears—but does not really hear.

The person who hears the *shofar* sound
And does not sense its call to change,
Hears—but does not really hear.

As the new year begins, O Lord,
Strengthen our ability to hear.

May we hear the music of the world,
And the infant's cry, and the lover's sigh.

May we hear the call for help of the lonely soul,
And the sound of the breaking heart.

May we hear the words of our friends,
And also their unspoken pleas and dreams.

May we hear within ourselves the yearnings
That are struggling for expression.

May we hear You, O God,

For only if we hear You
Do we have the right to hope
That You will hear us.

Hear the prayers we offer to You this day, O God,
And help us to hear them, too.

(Jack Riemer and Harold Kushner)

Renewal

Renewal is a focus of *Rosh Hashanah,* but in reality renewal is a year-round process. *Rosh Hashanah* reminds us of our having been created in God's image and of our power of renewal. God renews the world every day, and we renew ourselves in the world. We can be active in the renewal process. We have the capacity to renew ourselves—to make new those things that are repeated over and over in our lives.

In a way, *Rosh Hashanah* and *Yom Kippur* are atypical Jewish holidays. The primary observance of most festivals is in the home although there are always accompanying synagogue services. However, on the High Holy Days, while there are some home ceremonies, the focus of the observance is in the synagogue. While many Jews do not attend services regularly during the year and some Jews do not attend services at all, many Jews make certain to be present at this special season.

Because of the elevated tone of the prayers, the length of the services, and the large number of worshipers, there is a tendency for the High Holy Day services to be more formal than those on *Shabbat*. In addition to the prayers found in all Jewish services, special prayers dealing with the particular themes of the holidays are added. An example of this is the following prayer dealing with God's sovereignty, a major *Rosh Hashanah* theme:

Grant honor, God, to Your people, glory to those who revere You, hope to those who seek You, and courage to those who trust You; bless Your land with gladness and Your city with joy, and cause the light of redemption to dawn for all who dwell on earth.

Then the just shall see and exult, the upright be glad, and the faithful sing for joy. Violence shall rage no more, and evil shall vanish like smoke; the rule of tyranny shall pass away from the earth, and You alone, O God, shall have dominion over all Your works, as it is written: "God shall reign for ever; your God, O Zion, from generation to generation. Halleluyah!"

(Gates of Repentance, pp. 32–33)

There are distinctive melodies for much of the liturgy, and, when Jews hear these melodies, they are transported into a different dimension. The music evokes memories of past High Holy Days and links Jews with those generations that have gone before. Even for those new to the synagogue, the music in its own right can be very inspiring. The holiday prayers are found in a special prayer book called the *machzor*. Many congregations expect worshipers to provide their own *machzor* (in contrast to the year-round prayer book—the *siddur*—provided by the temple).

When one sits in *shul* (the synagogue) on *Rosh Hashanah,* the mind flashes back to the past—to childhood; to the events of the past year; to friends and family members, both absent and present. In the liturgy, *Rosh Hashanah* is called *Yom Hazikaron* (the Day of Remembrance), and truly it is a day for remembering.

We remember, too, the ancestors of the Jewish people, whose lives were exemplary. But it is not only we who remember; the liturgy speaks of God remembering as well.

Our God and God of all generations, remember us with favor and grant us Your compassionate deliverance. Remember Your love for us, the covenant You made with Abraham on Mount Moriah. Remember his boundless love for You, his willingness to offer You all that was his. Show us Your compassion, then, and in Your goodness look with favor upon Your people and Your loved ones. For You are the One who remembers all that has been forgotten; there is no forgetfulness in Your presence. Blessed is God, who remembers the covenant.

(Gates of Repentance, p. 146)

Customs

A traditional *Rosh Hashanah* afternoon ritual is called *Tashlich.* In this ceremony, conducted beside a body of moving water, Jews symbolically cast away their sins by throwing bread crumbs into the water. This is based on the statement of the prophet Micah (7:19): "And You [God] will cast [*vetashlich*] all their sins into the depths of the sea."

While the focus of the High Holy Days is congregational, there are traditions and customs that are observed at home. Since *Rosh Hashanah* is a day when Jews do not go to work or school, the holiday affords a wonderful opportunity for family and friends to be together. Customarily, a festive meal is eaten on *Rosh Hashanah* eve. Before this festival meal, candles are lit and the candlelighting blessings are recited. A special *Kiddush* (blessing over wine) is recited or chanted, and the *Motzi* (blessing over bread) is said over a round (often raisin) *chalah*. The traditional round shape of the *chalah* symbolizes the cycle of life. The eating of apples dipped in honey begins the meal, with a prayer that the new year will be sweet. Further extending this symbolism, sweet foods such as *kugel* and *tsimmes* are served at this meal, which often ends with honey cake and other sweets. Another custom is wearing new clothes in honor of the new year.

These customs are very beautiful and enrich our lives. They give us a framework to focus on self-assessment and personal and communal renewal, the compelling themes of *Rosh Hashanah*.

·3·

Seeking the Path of Life: Yom Kippur

Yom Kippur is the single holiest day of the Jewish year. It is a day of prayer, fasting, meditation, self-examination, and deep introspection— a day of moratorium on which we put aside all our normal activities and throw ourselves into the process of becoming one with God and the universe. *Yom Kippur* falls on the tenth day of the Hebrew month of *Tishri* and is the culmination of the High Holy Days. The commandment to observe this day is found in Leviticus 23:26–32. The Torah (Leviticus 23:32) states: "It shall be a sabbath of complete rest for you, and you shall practice self-denial; on the ninth day of the month at evening, from evening to evening, you shall observe this your sabbath."

Moratorium on the Everyday

This day is really different. It is a special kind of day off. When most people think of a day off, they think of taking it easy, relaxing. A day off implies vacation, but *Yom Kippur* is no vacation! It really is similar to taking inventory in a business. The store may be closed to the public on that day, but the people inside are still working hard. The process of taking stock requires serious attention. *Yom Kippur* is, in fact, a day of personal and spiritual inventory. While it is expected that spiritual stock-taking will be an ongoing process throughout the entire year, this one day is set aside and wholly dedicated to this purpose.

It has been said that an unexamined life is a life not worth living. *Yom Kippur* provides us with an opportunity for serious self-scrutiny. We take a day, put everything else out of our minds completely, and hold our lives up to a mirror. The idea is to see ourselves as God sees us.

Guilt

As we look into that mirror, we are bound to see imperfections. As we reflect on our actions of the past year, we focus on our shortcomings. This is likely to induce some feelings of guilt. Is this really so bad? It's very popular to say, "Don't lay a guilt trip on me." However, fairly assessed, guilt is not always crippling. It can be the impetus that causes us to examine our actions, thereby creating the healthy growth and development of our psyches.

Before guilt can produce a change in behavior, it must first produce a sense of estrangement—estrangement from others, estrangement from our own better selves, estrangement from God. There is a longing to break down the barriers, to draw near, to become at one—with the universe and with our true selves. At root, this is what *Yom Kippur,* the Day of At-one-ment, is all about.

Fasting

From biblical times, the practice of self-denial has been part of the *Yom Kippur* observance. The principal mode of self-denial is fasting. This is a complete fast, no food or drink from sunset to sunset. Who fasts? All Jews from the age of *Bar* and *Bat Mitzvah* are expected to fast, unless doing so will be health-threatening.

Beyond the fact that fasting is a religious obligation, there are additional dimensions to the practice. Some people fast as a concrete expression of the gravity of the day and of their state of mind. For others, fasting is a form of self-mastery. The goal of *Yom Kippur* is to assess our attitudes and behavior and strive to become better people. We need to prove to ourselves that we have control over ourselves and over our impulses. As a further emphasis on the moratorium aspect of the day, we fast as a means of focusing the mind on the spiritual. Fasting is also a means of awakening compassion. We are generally very well fed; many in the world go to bed hungry each night. Fasting is a reminder that others are in need, and it should motivate us to lend them our assistance. In fact, the day before *Yom Kippur* is tradition-ally a time for giving extra *tsedakah* as evidence of our sense of compas-sion.

Fasting is the primary way that we practice self-denial, but other forms of self-denial are also part of the traditional *Yom Kippur* obser-vance. Among these are abstinence from sex and from bathing for pleasure. Some Jews refrain from wearing shoes made of leather on *Yom Kippur*. One explanation for this is the incongruity of deriving benefit from the death of one of God's creatures while, at the same time, asking for life for ourselves. If you have ever wondered why, on *Yom Kippur*, you have seen men fully dressed with suits and ties but wearing tennis shoes, now you know!

Seeking Forgiveness

Yom Kippur, a day of introspection, is spent mostly in synagogue. The major themes of this day are reflected in the prayers specifically composed for this occasion.

One of the most important *Yom Kippur* prayers is *Al Chet* (For the sin . . .). It is a recounting of nearly every sin imaginable. Below is a shortened version of this prayer:

> The sin we have committed against
> You by malicious gossip,
>
> the sin we have committed against
> You by sexual immorality,
>
> and the sin we have committed
> against You by gluttony.
>
> The sin we have committed against
> You by narrow-mindedness,
>
> the sin we have committed against
> You by fraud and falsehood,
>
> and the sin we have committed
> against You by hating without
> cause.
>
> The sin we have committed against
> You by our arrogance,

the sin we have committed against
You by our insolence,

and the sin we have committed
against You by our irreverence.

The sin we have committed against
You by our hypocrisy,

the sin we have committed against
You by passing judgment on others,

and the sin we have committed
against You by exploiting the
weak.

The sin we have committed against
You by giving and taking bribes,

and the sin we have committed
against You by giving way to our
hostile impulses,

and the sin we have committed
against You by running to do evil.

For all these sins, O God of mercy,
forgive us, pardon us, grant us
atonement!
(*Gates of Repentance,* pp. 330–331)

You will notice that this prayer, like most prayers in Judaism, is written in the first person plural (we). At first, this may seem strange. You would expect a confession of sins to be written in the first person *singular* (I). Why the plural? It teaches us that we are part of a community and that we each share in communal responsibility. While it is highly unlikely that any one of us has committed every sin on the list, in our society all of these sins *have* been committed and are being committed, and we—as part of the society—bear some responsibility for what occurs. As Abraham Joshua Heschel has written: "In a free society, some are guilty, but all are responsible." This view of communal responsibility is contrary to the popular notion that individuals have no responsibility beyond themselves. Judaism stands firm on the principle that we are, indeed, responsible one for the other. The purpose of the prayer of confession is not to make us feel hopelessly guilty or sinful but, rather, to emphasize the magnitude of the responsibility we all bear.

There are many prayers that express the theme of *Yom Kippur*. One of the most beloved and significant is *Avinu Malkenu*. *Avinu Malkenu* (Our Father, our King) stresses two of God's attributes, immanence and transcendence. The prayer consists of many lines, each of which begins with the phrase *Avinu Malkenu* (Our Father, our King), and the final line can be translated: "Our Father, our King, be gracious to us and answer us even though we have not done all the good that we might have. Treat us generously and kindly, and be our help." We assert that God is the Creator of the whole universe and is sovereign over everything in it (transcendent). At the very same time, we conceive of God as very near to us like an ideal parent (immanent). For many Jews, hearing and singing the melody of *Avinu Malkenu* is one of the high points of the High Holy Day season.

While the prayers of *Yom Kippur* focus on asking God's forgiveness, that is really the second half of the process. The first half is seeking forgiveness from those people we may have hurt during the year. The classic teaching on this subject is found in *Mishnah Yoma* 8:9: "For sins between an individual and God, *Yom Kippur* can effect atonement; however, if a person has hurt another person, atonement is not possible until forgiveness of the wronged party has been sought." This teaching gave rise to the practice, prior to *Yom Kippur,* of actually approaching people whom we may have hurt during the year and asking forgiveness *from them.*

Preparation for Yom Kippur

This is only one of the ways we prepare for *Yom Kippur. Shabbat Shuvah* (Sabbath of Return), the Sabbath between *Rosh Hashanah* and *Yom Kippur,* offers another opportunity for preparation and introspection. *Shabbat Shuvah* is meant to be an integral part of the High Holy Days, and several special prayers are introduced into the liturgy to reinforce the holiday themes. This Sabbath takes its name from the *haftarah* (the selection from the Prophets that is read at Sabbath and festival services following the Torah reading) that begins with the word *Shuvah* ("Return [O Israel, to the Lord your God]"—Hosea 14:2).

While *Shabbat Shuvah* offers an opportunity for introspection and is meant to be an integral part of the holidays, the reality is that most people do not use this opportunity. They feel that they've just been through lengthy services on *Rosh Hashanah* and face even longer services on *Yom Kippur*. The result is that in many temples attendance on *Shabbat Shuvah* is small. What a far cry this is from the days of our great-grandparents by whom this was regarded as practically equal to the High Holy Days themselves. As a matter of fact, *Shabbat Shuvah* was one of the two times during the year that the rabbi would preach. (The other time was *Shabbat Hagadol*—the "Great Sabbath"—the Sabbath preceding Passover.) *Shabbat Shuvah* enables us to maintain spiritual momentum during the ten-day period of repentance, and it can be a very meaningful part of the season.

One preparatory custom that is widely observed is visiting the cemetery either before or during the High Holy Day period (though not on the Holidays themselves). Most Jewish communities have memorial services at the cemetery during this period. How does this help prepare for *Yom Kippur*? In reality, there are two ways. First, it reminds us of our mortality; recognizing that our time is limited, we are forced to assess ourselves on the deepest personal and spiritual levels. Second, visiting the graves of family members connects us with our past.

At times like these, we can feel very strongly the power of memory. Being Jewish is more than living in the present. We are aware that we are a part of a whole past that encompasses individuals and events that have gone before us. At the cemetery, as on *Yom Kippur*, we find ourselves suspended between the past and the future. We see that actively encountering our past empowers us to shape our future.

Synagogue Observance

This same feeling is with us on *Yom Kippur* itself when we participate in the *Yizkor* (memorial) service. During that service we remember those who were part of our personal lives. We also recall those whose lives have served as examples to us. Synagogues are usually crowded to capacity during *Yizkor* services. Even Jews who rarely attend synagogue want to participate in this hour of memory. It is the custom of some people whose parents are living to leave the sanctuary during the *Yizkor* service. Other people feel that this service is meaningful for them—even though their parents are living—and they remain in the temple.

Certainly, during the *Yizkor* service, the mood that fills the sanctuary is a sad one as people reflect upon their dear ones who have died.

However, the overall mood of *Yom Kippur* is *not* sad—it is solemn. Sitting in the sanctuary, one has the feeling that time is suspended. One really feels the moratorium aspects of this day because normal activities are not being done.

The mood of the day is heightened by the prevalence of white. The Torah scrolls are dressed in white. The reader's table is covered in white. The rabbis and cantors wear white robes. The wearing of white is not restricted to rabbis and cantors, however. Some congregants choose to wear white in keeping with the mood of the day. White, of course, is a symbol of purity. It is also intended to remind us of our mortality since white is the color of shrouds. In fact, on *Yom Kippur,* some people wear a *kittel,* one of the traditional Jewish burial garments. All this white serves to remind us that on *Yom Kippur* we reflect on the meaning of our lives while recognizing our mortality.

The mood of this holiday is set when we first enter the temple on *Yom Kippur* eve and hear the haunting melody of the *Kol Nidrei* chant. This melody draws Jews to the synagogue.

Yom Kippur ends with a very dramatic service called *Neilah* (closing). The allusion is to the "closing of the gates," variously interpreted as the closing of the gates of the ancient Temple in Jerusalem or the closing of the very gates of heaven. The service concludes with a final blast of the *shofar*. Among the worshipers, there is a feeling of exhilaration as this great day draws to a close, and they prepare to break the fast with family and friends.

Home Observance

More than on any other holiday, the focus of *Yom Kippur* is the synagogue. The home observances of *Yom Kippur* consist of a prefast meal and a meal to break the fast.

At their prefast meal, many people prefer to eat foods that are not heavily spiced or salted so that they will not be inordinately thirsty during the hours of the fast. Following the prefast meal, *yahrzeit* candles are lit in memory of the departed, and candles are kindled in honor of the holiday. The candles are lit after the meal rather than before (as is usual on *Shabbat* and other holidays) because, once the candle blessings have been said, the holiday has begun and eating is inappropriate. Once the candles have been lit, people go to the synagogue for *Kol Nidrei,* and the synagogue then remains the focus of observance for the next twenty-four hours.

Turning and Returning

So what is the purpose of all this? What are the High Holy Days supposed to accomplish? Do we really expect to become perfect? What impact can all these hours of services really have on us and our lives?

In order for the High Holy Days to be more than an aesthetic or nostalgic experience, we have to have been touched deeply and changed somehow by our encounter with this season. We are not talking about blinding flashes of insight or earthshaking revelations. Often the changes are subtle and almost imperceptible; sometimes we recognize them only in retrospect. The changes are the result of that process we have referred to as *teshuvah*.

This process can be likened to physical exercise. When we first begin, we are out of condition, we may not know the proper techniques, and we are not in touch with our bodies. But, as we continue, we gradually get into condition, we learn the techniques, and we are put in touch with our bodies. Each time, we reach a little higher, we try a little harder, we grow a little stronger.

The process of *teshuvah* is *spiritual* exercise. We have to *train* ourselves to approach this season and this frame of mind. In beginning our training, we place ourselves on a path. We don't travel the entire path in one year's time. However, each year we are a little farther along; we know a little more about ourselves. As a result of being on this path, we clarify our values, and we aim at certain goals. We judge our progress through periodic self-assessment all along the path, but especially at certain peak points in our journey. The High Holy Days provide a major stopping point to analyze how far we have come.

MAJOR FESTIVALS

·4·

Permanence and Fragility: Sukot

When many Jews say "the Holidays" they mean *Rosh Hashanah* and *Yom Kippur*. In fact, there are other fall holidays! Just five days after *Yom Kippur* (on the fifteenth day of the Hebrew month of *Tishri*), *Sukot* begins. It is a week-long harvest festival known in Jewish tradition as *Zeman Simchatenu* (the Season of Our Joy). It is truly a happy and a beautiful holiday with elements appealing to the various senses. Long neglected, in recent years this holiday has become more widely observed.

Sukot is one of the three Pilgrimage Festivals (the others being *Pesach* and *Shavuot*) commanded by the Bible. On each of these harvest festivals, our ancestors would make a pilgrimage to the Temple in Jerusalem to make a festival offering. Because this holiday is commanded in the Torah, it is considered a major festival. There are really two strands that run through the holiday of *Sukot*—one is the agricultural and the other is the historical.

Ritual and observance are often reenactments of historical events. During *Sukot*, we commemorate the forty years the Israelites wandered in the desert after the Exodus from Egypt. We relive and re-create their fragile surroundings, their lack of a sturdy home, and the precariousness of their existence.

Building a Sukah

To celebrate this holiday, we build a *sukah* outside our synagogue. Many people build one at home as well. The plural of *sukah* is *sukot*, from which the holiday takes its name. A *sukah* is a temporary structure, usually with three sides, high enough for a person to stand in, covered with cut branches, and decorated with hanging fruits and vegetables. Sometimes *sukot* are large and rather elaborate; sometimes they are small and quite simple.

Links to Our Past

As we sit in a *sukah,* we feel linked to our ancestors who lived in temporary dwellings during their journey to the Promised Land. The Bible reminds us: "You shall live [sit] in booths [*sukot*] seven days . . . in order that future generations may know that I made the Israelite people live in booths [*sukot*] when I brought them out of the land of Egypt, I the Lord your God." (Leviticus 23:42–43) Furthermore, sitting in a fragile structure like a *sukah* gives us a chance to reflect upon the fragile nature of life itself.

Upon entering the *sukah,* it is customary to bless God for having given us the *mitzvah* of sitting in the *sukah.* On the eve of the holiday, the meal is preceded by blessing the festival candles, by chanting the festival *Kiddush,* and by reciting the *Motzi.* During the holiday, we eat our meals in the *sukah.* Some people even sleep in it. While there is no one food universally eaten on *Sukot,* stuffed vegetables are very common as are other foods made from vegetables and fruits, in keeping with the harvest nature of the holiday.

One lovely *Sukot* tradition is inviting guests to the *sukah.* In general, hospitality (*hachnasat orechim*) is both a *mitzvah* and a cherished Jewish value. We have heard many stories and personally had experiences of strangers coming to a synagogue for the first time and being invited to people's homes for a *Shabbat* or festival meal. This is particularly appropriate on *Sukot,* when we express our thanks for the bounty which is ours. Another way to show our appreciation for our blessings is to think of those in need and share with them. Many congregations sponsor canned food drives during *Sukot* (and ongoing drives during the year).

Another form of hospitality is to invite guests from the Jewish past into our *sukah.* We welcome Abraham and Sarah, Isaac and Rebekah, etc. These guests are called *ushpizin.* By invoking the memory of these heroic figures, we are living on two planes—the present and the past.

"Meal of the Jews during the Feast of the Tents," Bernard Picart; Holland, early 18th century. From the collection of the Hebrew Union College Skirball Museum.

Sukot brings to mind, not only the Jewish past, but the American past as well. Many people believe that the American holiday of Thanksgiving is based on *Sukot*. The Pilgrims were great Bible readers and may well have used the biblical *Sukot* as a model for their harvest celebration.

Lulav and Etrog

The agricultural strand of *Sukot* is symbolized by the use of a *lulav* and *etrog*. A *lulav* is a dried palm branch, which has attached to it, in a holder at its base, sprigs of myrtle and willow. An *etrog* is a citron, a rather uncommon member of the citrus family that looks like a lemon. The palm, myrtle, willow, and citron are sometimes referred to as the Four Species (*Arba'ah Minim*). The biblical basis for using these items is found in Leviticus 23:40: "On the first day you shall take the product of *hadar* [goodly] trees, branches of palm trees, boughs of leafy trees, and willows of the brook, and you shall rejoice before the Lord your God seven days." While this verse mentions the palm and willow by name, how do we arrive at the use of the myrtle and citron? These are derived from rabbinic interpretations found in the Talmud. One

Etrog box; Germany, 19th century. From the collection of the Hebrew Union College Skirball Museum, photography by John R. Forsman.

of the talmudic passages informs us that the citron was selected as the "product of the goodly trees [*hadar*], only after the bark of many trees was sampled to determine which tasted the 'goodliest.'"

A blessing is recited when the *lulav* and *etrog* are held. We then shake the *lulav* and *etrog* in all directions to symbolize that God is everywhere. The *lulav* and *etrog* can be purchased in a Jewish book store or a store that specializes in Jewish religious articles. While synagogues generally have a *lulav* and *etrog* available for people to use, some individuals prefer to purchase their own. Putting the *etrog* into a lovely case can enhance the celebration of the holiday. Indeed, throughout many centuries, Jewish artistic creativity has found expression in exquisite *etrog* boxes.

A number of interpretations have been offered for the *lulav* and *etrog*. One of these is based on the shape of each of the Four Species. The *lulav*, which looks like a spine, symbolizes action and courage. The *etrog*, which looks like a heart, symbolizes feelings. The myrtle, the leaf of which resembles an eye, symbolizes awareness and understanding. The willow, the leaf of which resembles a mouth, symbolizes truth.

Another interpretation, rather than basing itself on the shape of each of the Four Species, uses the properties of each to point to a deeper meaning of the ritual. Likening fragrance to good deeds and taste to learning, it examines each of the species: the willow, which has neither taste nor fragrance, symbolizes the Jew who has neither learning nor good deeds; the myrtle, which has fragrance but no taste, stands for the Jew who does good deeds but has no learning; the palm, the fruit of which has taste but no fragrance, symbolizes the Jew who is learned but does not act upon his learning; and the *etrog,* which has both taste and fragrance, stands for the ideal Jew, a person who possesses learning and actively pursues goodness.

Synagogue Observance

There are synagogue services for *Sukot,* where you may see processions (*hakafot*) of people carrying their *lulav* and *etrog* around the sanctuary. During the singing or recitation of the *Hallel* (special psalms of praise), the *lulav* and *etrog* are shaken.

During the holiday, we read the biblical Book of Ecclesiastes. This is one of five books historically kept in scroll form (the word for scroll in Hebrew is *megillah;* the plural is *megillot*), which are read on different holidays: Ecclesiastes (*Kohelet*) is read on *Sukot;* Esther is read on *Purim;* Song of Songs (*Shir Hashirim*) is read on *Pesach;* Ruth is read on *Shavuot;* and Lamentations (*Echah*) is read on the Fast of the Ninth of Av (*Tishah Be'av*).

Tradition ascribes the authorship of three biblical books to King Solomon. The content and tone of each has led commentators to imagine that the books were written at different stages of Solomon's life: Song of Songs in his youth, Proverbs (*Mishlei*) when he had gained maturity, and Ecclesiastes in his old age. *Kohelet,* sometimes called "the gentle cynic," seems to speak very much to the situation in our own time.

In the Talmud, *Sukot* is referred to as *Hechag,* the Holiday—the Holiday *par excellence.* This is a holiday that engages the whole person: It is a delight to the senses, an awakener of the memory, and an inspiration for the soul. In our day, it can and should become—once again—the Holiday *par excellence.*

·5·

Torah as Our Source of Joy: Simchat Torah

Simchat Torah (literally, the joy of the Torah) is a holiday at the end of *Sukot*. In order to discuss this holiday we should have an understanding of just what Torah is.

Meaning of Torah

The word "Torah" is sometimes translated as "the Law," and that translation is certainly not incorrect; on the other hand, it only begins to tell the story. The word "teaching" probably captures the richness of association that the concept "Torah" brings with it. Torah has both a narrow and a broad sense. In its narrowest sense, it is the Pentateuch—the Five Books of Moses—the first five books of the Bible. In the broader sense, Torah encompasses everything that flows from the Pentateuch, from the other books of the Bible, to the words of the ancient rabbinic sages, and to the writings of inspired teachers. In other words, Torah really means Judaism. Thus, Torah is central to Jewish life—as an object, as our history and folklore, as our law, as a statement of our ethical values, as a symbol of our relationship to God.

If you hear Jews say that they are "studying Torah," it might not necessarily mean that they are delving, for example, into the Book of Exodus. It could mean that they are learning a tractate of Talmud or

·41

a commentary. Study is integral to Jewish life. The Jewish tradition has always valued study, and the learned person has historically had a place of honor in the community. In fact, study was so important that it was not considerd just a leisure-time activity but, rather, the primary occupation of the Jew. People were expected to set aside time to study every day. Because the first-century sage Hillel believed this but at the same time understood human nature, he advised: "Do not say, 'When I have leisure I shall study [Torah]—you may never have any leisure.' "

What is the relationship of the Torah to the Bible? The Torah is the first part of the Bible. The Bible is sometimes referred to as the Holy Scriptures or the Hebrew Scriptures. Another term for Bible is actually an acronym—*TaNaCH*. It consists of the first letter of the three sections into which Jews divide the biblical books—namely, *Torah*, *Nevi'im* (Prophets), and *Ketuvim* (Writings).

However, there is one term that we do not use for the Bible. We never call our Bible the "Old Testament." This may seem strange since the books of our Bible are exactly the same books that would be contained in the Old Testament section of a Christian Bible. (The Catholic Church recognizes the apocryphal books as part of the Old Testament while the Protestant denominations do not. Judaism historically has not recognized the Apocrypha as part of the Bible.) So why don't we call our Bible the "Old Testament"?

In biblical language, "testament" has the connotation of "covenant." We believe that the covenant made between God and Abraham and Abraham's descendants is eternally valid and unsupplantable. If Jews were to use the term "Old Testament," it would imply that in our religion there is a "New Testament" and that the "Old Testament" is only part of the story.

Torah Customs

Often when people speak of "the Torah," they are referring to an actual parchment scroll on which the Five Books of Moses are written by hand. The parchment comes from the skin of a kosher animal and the letters are inscribed with a quill pen by a specially trained scribe called a *sofer*. In the synagogue, the Torah scroll (*sefer Torah*) is kept in a special cabinet called the *Aron Hakodesh* (the Holy Ark). As a sign of our love and reverence for the Torah, we adorn it with a mantle of fine velvet or silk, often embroidered or decorated, and with an

Detail of a menorah, Torah ark door; Poland, early 18th century. From the collection of the Hebrew Union College Skirball Museum, photography by John R. Forsman.

ornamental silver breastplate and crowns. We also place on the Torah a silver pointer called a *yad* (literally, hand). The *yad* is used by Torah readers to keep their place while reading the scroll. This is particularly necessary because the *sefer Torah* is written without vowels or punctuation.

Before the Torah is read, the crowns, the *yad,* the breastplate, and the mantle are taken off. We call this "undressing" the Torah. After the Torah reading, we "dress" the Torah. It is an honor to be called to the *bimah* (the raised platform in the synagogue from which the service is led) to dress or undress the Torah.

While the overwhelming number of synagogues in North America follow Ashkenazic (Central/Eastern European) customs, there are a num-

Rimonim; Frankfurt, Germany, c.a. 1750. From the collection of the Hebrew Union College Skirball Museum.

ber of congregations that observe Sephardic (Southern European/North African/Middle Eastern) practices. In Sephardic synagogues, for instance, the Holy Ark is known as the *Heichal* and the raised platform is called the *tevah*. Sephardic Torahs are contained in artistically crafted cases.

It must appear somewhat strange to someone who walks into the synagogue for the first time to see how people relate to the Torah. In many congregations, the dressed Torah scroll is carried around the sanctuary in a procession (*hakafah*) before and after it is read. As the Torah passes by, many people kiss the Torah directly or indirectly by touching it with their prayer book or *talit* and then kissing that object. Why? It's simply a way of showing love and respect. It is important to note that, while a great deal of love is shown for the Torah, it is not considered an object of veneration or worship. (Another way that we show respect for our holy books, in addition to studying them, of course, is by never putting them on the floor. As a matter of fact, when they are accidentally dropped, it is customary to kiss them when we pick them up.)

The Torah is read each week at services. The selections read follow a set cycle so that, traditionally, the entire Torah is read during the course of one year. The terms used for this weekly Torah portion are *parashah, sidrah,* or *sedrah.* Most Jewish calendars list the name of the Torah portion on the Sabbath of each week. Blessings are recited before and after the Torah is read. In many congregations, one or more individuals are called to the *bimah,* usually by their Hebrew names, for the honor of reciting or chanting these blessings. This honor is called an *aliyah* (literally, a going up).

We have two holidays centering on the Torah—*Shavuot* and *Simchat Torah. Shavuot* marks the historical event of the Jewish people receiving the Torah at Mount Sinai while *Simchat Torah* celebrates the completion of the annual reading of the Torah. On *Simchat Torah* we read the final portion of Deuteronomy and immediately read the first portion of Genesis. In this way we demonstrate that the study of Torah never ceases.

Synagogue Observance

Prior to reading from the Torah on *Simchat Torah,* all of the Torah scrolls (most synagogues have more than one) are removed from the ark and carried around the sanctuary in a series of joyous *hakafot* (processionals). (Traditionally, there are seven *hakafot.*) In many synagogues, the honor of carrying the Torahs is extended to all Jews above *Bar/Bat Mitzvah* age. The Torah carriers lead the procession, followed by numerous adults and children carrying special *Simchat Torah* flags. During the *hakafot,* songs are sung, and there is often joyous dancing. In fact, in some synagogues each *hakafah* ends with groups of people dancing joyously in a circle, at the center of which are the Torah scrolls held aloft.

After the *hakafot,* the Torah is read. The person called to recite or chant the blessings over the final section of the Torah is called the *Chatan Torah* (bridegroom of the Torah) and the person who recites or chants the blessings over the first section of the Torah is called *Chatan Bereshit* (bridegroom of Genesis). In synagogues where women are called to the Torah, the honorees are called *Kalat Torah* (bride of the Torah) and *Kalat Bereshit* (bride of Genesis). These terms indicate that the relationship between God and the people of Israel can be compared to that of a husband and wife. The Torah, then, is the *ketubah* (marriage contract) and *Simchat Torah* can be seen as an anniversary celebration. The back-to-back reading of the end of Deuteronomy and the beginning of Genesis underscores the idea that Torah study is to be continuous, never allowed to stop.

In some congregations, it is customary to call every adult to the *bimah* for an *aliyah* over the final portion of Deuteronomy. (In Orthodox congregations, only men are called to the Torah; in Reform and Reconstructionist, both men and women are called; in Conservative, customs vary.) Often the adults come up in groups. Afterwards, all the children come to the *bimah* together. A large *talit* is held over the group as an adult leads them in the Torah blessings.

Growing out of this custom is the Reform-originated ceremony of Consecration. This ceremony marks the beginning of formal Jewish studies for small children. During the *Simchat Torah* service, the children are called to the *bimah* and, often, a *talit* is held over them as they receive a special blessing from the rabbi. They are also presented with their own miniature Torah scrolls. It is appropriate that on the day of celebrating the joy of Torah we officially welcome the new generation of Torah learners.

Unlike many other Jewish holidays observed mainly in the home, *Simchat Torah* is celebrated primarily in the synagogue. The only home aspects of the holiday are the candlelighting, the *Kiddush,* and the *Motzi* over the *chalah,* which are done at home before the festival meal prior to going to services.

Simchat Torah is a holiday of postbiblical origin. It began as a way of celebrating the second day of the biblically ordained festival of *Shemini Atseret,* which concludes the *Sukot* season. In most Reform congregations and in Israel, *Shemini Atseret* and *Simchat Torah* are combined.

In our time, *Simchat Torah* has become an occasion to focus attention on the plight of Soviet Jewry. By dedicating one *hakafah* to those Jews in the Soviet Union that have been denied the right to emigrate we show our solidarity with them. Other ways of showing our solidarity include marching outside the synagogue with Torah scrolls, banners, and placards; sending postcards and letters of protest to the Soviet government, to the United States government, and to the United Nations; and sending notes of encouragement to those Jews in the Soviet Union facing extra persecution because they have applied for exit visas and been refused (*refuseniks*). The reason for the connection between

Simchat Torah and Soviet Jewry is that it is on *Simchat Torah* that tens of thousands of Soviet Jews, both young and old, congregate inside and outside the synagogues to assert their Jewish identity with pride. Not only is this an act of Jewish affirmation, in Russia this is an act of courage and defiance since the government is officially antireligious and unofficially anti-Semitic. For decades the Soviet government has systematically endeavored to put an end to Jewish cultural life. Of late, there has been a lessening of these restrictions, which we hope will now make Jewish life easier in the Soviet Union.

The Torah is a symbol of those values that Jews hold most dear. It provides guidance and inspiration for our lives. *Simchat Torah* is our way of celebrating the continuity of Torah in our lives and acknowledging the joy that it brings us.

· 6 ·

Redemption and Freedom: Pesach

Pesach (Passover) was ordained in the Bible as an annual week-long festival commemorating the Exodus from Egypt. The holiday derives its name from the passing over of the homes of the Israelite slaves during the tenth plague. In biblical times, it also marked the spring harvest. Today, in Israel, Passover is observed for seven days. Outside of Israel, Orthodox and Conservative Jews observe this holiday for eight days while most Reform Jews observe it for seven days. The holiday begins on the fifteenth day of the Hebrew month of *Nisan*.

It has often been said that Judaism is a home-centered religion. At no time of the year is this more obvious than at *Pesach*. The *seder,* the high point of the festival observance, is the ultimate home ceremony.

Family and friends gather together on the first night of the holiday for a wonderful feast. But the *seder* is more than an elaborate dinner party. It is more than the sum total of all the dishes that are served. It is both a retelling and a reliving of the Exodus experience. Through story and song, through tasting of symbolic foods, and through sharing of common memories, the historical and contemporary meanings of freedom are explored by young and old around the *seder* table. Many Jews observe the *seder* on two nights.

The Meaning of the Seder

The word *seder* means "order." There is a definite order to the various rituals of the *seder*. Participants follow the ceremony from a special book that contains the prayers, the songs, and the story of Passover. The book is called a *haggadah,* which means "telling."

This joyous holiday of Passover is most fully appreciated when it is shared. Indeed, it is considered a *mitzvah* to extend hospitality by inviting guests to the *seder*. A well-known passage in the *haggadah* says: "May all in need come and celebrate Passover with us." The phrase "all in need" often brings to mind people in financial need. (Most Jewish communities have a *Maot Chitim* fund that provides Passover necessities for the needy.) We also have to remember that there are other kinds of need. People may be in need of companionship, of friendship, of community. There may be people who have just moved into the community or who are new to Judaism. Our *seder* celebration with family and friends is enriched by involving all these. Many synagogues hold a community *seder* (often on the second night).

The *seder* is the central element in the celebration of this holiday. People sit around a festively laid table as the pageant of history unfolds. A special effort is made to have the table look as beautiful as possible. A ceremonial *seder* plate is set in front of the leader. Placed upon it are the various symbols of the *seder:* a roasted shankbone for the ancient paschal offering, a green herb or vegetable representing spring, a roasted egg symbolizing the additional offering made in biblical times specifically for holidays, *charoset* (a paste-like mixture of fruits, nuts, and wine) reminding us of the mortar used by the slaves, and a bitter herb like horseradish for the bitterness of slavery. A special goblet, set aside for the prophet Elijah, is placed on the table. In addition to the *matzah* to be eaten during the course of the meal, three ceremonial *matzot* are placed on the table before the leader. These represent the two traditional loaves set out in the ancient Temple during the festival day and the extra *matzah* symbolic of Passover. Eating *matzah* (flat cracker-like unleavened bread) during the *seder* is a reminder of the haste with which the slaves left Egypt. They had no time to wait for the bread to rise. It also symbolizes the poor fare that the slaves had to eat. Today, many people set out a fourth *matzah,* usually referred to as "the *matzah* of hope," as a reminder of those Jews in many lands who are not yet allowed to live in freedom.

The Elements of the Seder

In many homes, the *seder* begins with the lighting of candles; in other homes, the custom is to light them earlier, just prior to sunset. Two blessings are recited over the candles to mark the beginning of the holiday.

During the *seder,* every participant drinks four cups of wine, each cup at a specified point in the service. The four cups represent the four promises of redemption made by God to the Israelites: "I will *free* you from the burdens of the Egyptians and *deliver* you from their bondage. I will *redeem* you with an outstretched arm and through extraordinary chastisements. And I will *take* you to be My people." (Exodus 6:6–7)

In biblical times, Passover was the spring harvest festival. A reminder of this in the *seder* is the eating of *karpas* (a green herb like parsley or a green vegetable such as celery or watercress). The green is dipped in salt water, a symbol of the tears shed by our enslaved ancestors.

Breaking the middle *matzah* of the ceremonial *matzot* is called *yachats.* The middle *matzah* is broken and half of it, called the *afikoman,* is hidden by the leader (or "stolen" by the children), to be found after the meal. The *afikoman* is the last thing to be eaten, and the *seder* cannot continue until it is found. The children hold the *afikoman* for ransom and are given a reward for returning it. This is one of the ways the children are involved in the *seder.*

Children play an important part in the *seder.* Near the beginning of the *seder,* the youngest child present asks the traditional Four Questions:

> Why is this night different from all other nights?
>
> On all other nights we eat leavened or unleavened bread; tonight why do we eat only unleavened?
>
> On all other nights we eat all kinds of vegetables; tonight why do we eat only bitter herbs?
>
> On all other nights we are not required to dip at our meal; tonight why do we dip two times?
>
> On all other nights we eat either seated upright or reclining; tonight why do we all recline?

The remainder of the *seder* is really a response to those questions.

The retelling of the Exodus story is a *mitzvah.* We are told that, the more we expound upon the story of the Exodus, the more deserving of praise we are. The retelling of the Exodus experience begins with the memory of the enslavement of the Israelites in Egypt. The narrative progresses from slavery to freedom, from degradation to dignity.

The *seder,* however, is more than a recapitulation of history. Through its stories and examples, we learn values and ideals. For instance, the *haggadah* speaks of four children (the Hebrew word *banim* can be translated as "sons" or "children," but editors of modern *haggadah*s, sensitive to gender issues, translate it as "children"): the wise, the wicked, the simple, and the one who does not know how to ask. What distinguishes the wise from the wicked? The wise includes himself or herself in the ceremonies while the wicked excludes himself or herself by sneeringly asking, "What is this observance to *you*?" A cardinal Jewish value is participating in the life of the Jewish community. As the ancient sage Hillel taught: "Do not separate yourself from the community."

As part of the retelling of the Exodus story, we recount the ten plagues that were visited upon the Egyptians. As we mention each plague, we remove a drop of wine from our cup. A full cup would symbolize complete joy. By diminishing the amount of wine in the cup, we symbolically show that our joy is diminished when other people suffer. A well-known *midrash* says that, when the Israelites crossed the Sea of Reeds into freedom, they sang a song of rejoicing and were joined by an angelic chorus. At that moment, God chastised the angels by saying: "How can you sing while My children [the Egyptians] are drowning in the sea!"

Although saddened by the suffering of those who perished in the sea, we rejoice in the freedom that is ours. One of the most popular songs of the *seder* is *Dayenu,* which means "It would have been enough for us." The song recounts the various blessings that God bestowed upon us, such as our freedom, the Torah, the Sabbath, and the land of Israel.

The key to understanding what the *seder* is really all about is found in this *haggadah* passage: "In every generation each person is obligated to see himself or herself as if he or she went forth from Egypt." As we sit around the *seder* table, we are transported back to the time when we were slaves in Egypt. We not only read about our ancestors, we become one with them. We experience leaving Egypt, the passing through the Sea of Reeds, and the beginning of the march toward Sinai and toward the Promised Land.

When we sit at the *seder* table, we are linked, not only to our ancestors who left Egypt, but also to those of every successive generation who have relived the experience in quite the same way. We feel the unity that comes from Jews throughout the world celebrating *Pesach* at the same time. We are united by deep and powerful memories. In this generation, at some point in the *seder,* we especially recall the events of the Holocaust. We remember that it was during *Pesach* that the heroic uprising of the Warsaw Ghetto began. We connect ourselves to those events by specially chosen readings and by the singing of *Ani Ma'amin,* which had been sung by many on their way to death in the concentration camps.

While, on Passover, we realize that Jewish life is filled with both sadness and joy, the prevailing mood of the *seder* is joyous. One of the ways we give expression to the joy we feel at this special time is by *Hallel,* part of which is recited or sung before dinner and part after. The word *hallel* means "praise." The English word "halleluyah" actually comes from the Hebrew *hallelu Yah* (praise God), which incorporates a plural form of the word *hallel* with one of the names for God. *Hallel* is one of the oldest sections of the *haggadah.* It is taken from the Bible and consists of Psalms 113–118. *Hallel* is associated with certain Jewish festivals. It is part of the synagogue service on *Pesach, Shavuot, Sukot,* and *Chanukah.*

Probably one of the best-remembered elements of the *seder* is that point at which a child is asked to open the door for the prophet Elijah. According to tradition, Elijah is the forerunner of the Messiah, who will bring ultimate redemption. Since Passover is a holiday that celebrates freedom, our thoughts turn particularly to redemption and Elijah. We set out a special cup for Elijah, which remains untouched during the *seder.* Some people follow the custom of having those around the *seder* table pour a little wine from their glasses into Elijah's cup, symbolically affirming individual commitment to the goal of building a better world. We open the door to welcome symbolically the spirit of Elijah. One explanation for the origin of the custom of opening the door is that, during the Middle Ages, groundless accusations were made that Jews used the blood of Christian children to make *matzah.* This accusation is called the "blood libel." The door was opened to show publicly that the *seder* was a normal family celebration of a holiday.

Festival Observance

The *seder* itself, though it is the high point of the holiday, is by no means the totality of our observance of Passover. For a week, we are

Seder container; Vienna, Austria, 1815. From the collection of the Hebrew Union College Skirball Museum, photography by Marvin Rand.

reminded of the Exodus from Egypt by eating *matzah* (unleavened bread) rather than our more normal, leavened bread. There are many levels of Passover observance within the Jewish community. The spectrum ranges from those Jews who simply refrain from eating leavened bread to those who eat only foods specially designated for Passover and use utensils and dishes completely different from those used during the rest of the year. Most Jews prepare for Passover by engaging in a thorough spring cleaning.

While *Pesach* is observed primarily at home, it is observed in the synagogue as well. On the Sabbath preceding *Pesach,* known as *Shabbat Hagadol* (the Great Sabbath), a special *haftarah* (prophetic selection) is read. This *haftarah* mentions the sending of the prophet Elijah before the *great* day of God. Festival services are held on the first and last days of the holiday. In many congregations, the *Yizkor* (memorial) prayers are part of the services on the concluding day.

There is much to be said about *Pesach.* Its greatness lies not only in the significant event of the past that it commemorates but also in the sense of connectedness with our people and in the personal renewal that it inspires in us.

> This is the day that the Lord has made—
> let us exult and rejoice on it.
> (Psalm 118:24 from *Hallel*)

·7·

Torah as Our Source of Strength: Shavuot

Shavuot, the Festival of Weeks, occurs on the sixth day of the Hebrew month of *Sivan*—seven weeks after the beginning of Passover. In biblical times, it was the end-of-spring harvest festival on which the first fruits of the season were offered in the Temple in Jerusalem. For this reason, it was called *Chag Habikurim* (Festival of the First Fruits). It was one of the three Pilgrimage Festivals (the other two being *Pesach* and *Sukot*) during which our ancestors made their way to Jerusalem to celebrate the holiday in the Temple. As a commemoration of the original harvest-nature of the festival, it has become customary to decorate our synagogues and homes with flowers or plants on this holiday.

Synagogue Observance

Shavuot is also known as *Zeman Matan Toratenu* (the Season of the Giving of Our Torah). It marks the anniversary of our receiving the Ten Commandments and, by extension, the Torah. The Torah reading on this holiday is, therefore, the Ten Commandments. The Book of Ruth is also read on *Shavuot.* There are two reasons for this: first, an important part of Ruth's story unfolds during the harvest season; second, Ruth voluntarily accepted the Torah. Not born Jewish, she became a Jew by choice. Indeed, she is the first recorded convert to Judaism.

A major feature of *Shavuot* services in Reform, many Conservative, and some modern Orthodox synagogues is the ceremony of Confirmation. This is a group ceremony in which a class (usually, the tenth grade) marks the completion of a prescribed course of study in a temple school. The youngsters are confirming their intention to live their lives as Jews. The Confirmation ceremony may include the reading from the Torah, a cantata or drama, special music, speeches, a floral offering, and the blessing of the confirmands by the rabbi.

Customs

Shavuot is welcomed at home with a festival meal, beginning with blessings over candles, wine, and *chalah*. Dairy products are often eaten on *Shavuot* since the Bible compares the Torah to milk and honey. A favorite dairy dish among *Ashkenazim* (Jews of Central and Eastern European background) is *blintzes* (cheese-filled crêpes).

A long-established *Shavuot* custom is engaging in all-night study on *Shavuot* eve. This custom has not been widely observed by non-Orthodox Jews, but in recent years it is beginning to be revived. Some synagogues conduct study sessions using a book called *Tikkun Leil Shavuot* (*Service of the Night of Shavuot*). It is an anthology that includes the opening and closing verses of each weekly Pentateuch portion and of every other biblical book, the entire Scroll of Ruth, the first and last few passages of each tractate of the Mishnah, and selections from mystical works. Some Jews gather in private homes for all or part of the night to study on *Shavuot* eve and follow their own study program based on their interests.

While the celebration of *Shavuot* includes many lovely customs, it is first and foremost a commemoration of the giving of the Torah. In Judaism, Torah is seen as evidence of God's love. We recognize that for people to live together in society there is a need for law. Laws are basic and fundamental to Torah and are needed to ensure harmonious living. Jewish tradition views the gift of Torah as a loving one. Indeed, Torah is the guiding principle of Jewish life.

Though the Ten Commandments were given to the Jewish people, Judaism sees them as having universal application. A number of *midrashim* (the ancient rabbis' "reading between the lines" of the biblical text) make this point. One *midrash* states that, when the commandments were given, there was complete silence in the *entire universe*. Another points out that the place of revelation was Sinai—in the middle of the desert—in a "no-man's land." This was to teach that the laws are for everyone.

The Sinai experience touched all Jews. There is a *midrash* that says that *all* Jewish souls—past, present, and future (including those who would choose to become Jewish)—were present at Sinai. All Jews are bound together, and the memory of the Sinai experience is one of the important ties that bind us.

Revelation

We cannot talk about Torah without saying something about revelation. By revelation, we mean ways in which God is revealed to people. The basic underlying difference between the Orthodox and non-Orthodox approaches to Judaism hinges on this very issue. Many people think that the differences center around the wearing of a head covering or the use of Hebrew in worship. These are only outward signs. Indeed, a non-Orthodox Jew (Conservative, Reform, Reconstructionist) might pray in Hebrew and wear a *yarmulke*. That would not make that Jew Orthodox!

So, what is the real distinction between these approaches to Judaism (and that is exactly what they are—different approaches rather than different denominations)? The Orthodox view is that everything in the Torah (both the material in the Five Books of Moses and the ancient rabbis' interpretations of that material) was revealed directly by God. The non-Orthodox view is that the Torah contains the understanding of many people about God. It evolved over a long period of time and was written by numerous individuals. There are a variety of opinions concerning revelation among Reform, Reconstructionist, and Conservative scholars. Some speak in terms of "progressive revelation" (the idea that God is revealed differently in every age); others say that Torah *contains* the word of God rather than *is* the word of God. All agree, however, that it is the basis of our code of moral action.

Classic Jewish Sources

As we have previously noted in Chapter 5, the word "Torah" is used in a narrow sense and in a broad sense. In a narrow sense, it refers to the Pentateuch—the first five books of the Bible. In a broad sense, it is used to mean everything that flows from the Pentateuch, including—but not limited to—the rest of the Bible, the Talmud, and the Midrash. A word should be said about each of these.

The Bible, also known as the Holy Scriptures, is divided into three sections: *Torah* (Teaching), *Nevi'im* (Prophets), and *Ketuvim* (Writings). A popular way of referring to the Bible is the term *TaNaCH*, a word made up of the first letters of each of the three sections. When Jews speak about the Bible, we are referring to the collection of books that is known in the Christian community as the "Old Testament."

The Talmud is a record of the ancient rabbis' grappling with the laws of the Bible in an attempt to understand them and apply them to the conditions of life that they faced. It is made up of two parts, *Mishnah* and *Gemara*. The *Mishnah* is a code of Jewish law, developed over many generations and edited by Rabbi Judah Ha-Nasi around the year 200 C.E. The *Gemara* is a collection of legal and ethical discussions of the rabbis of the third through fifth centuries. The Talmud was edited around the year 500 C.E.

The Midrash consists of collections of works, compiled between the third and twelfth centuries, that seek to explicate the underlying truths and meanings of the biblical text.

One of the early talmudic sages, Rabbi Simon the Just, is quoted as saying: "The world stands on three things—on Torah, on worship, and on acts of lovingkindness." Most certainly, the world of Judaism stands on these three pillars. On the festival of *Shavuot,* the Season of the Giving of our Torah, we are reminded of the centrality of Torah, which teaches us to worship God through our kind and fair dealings with all of God's creatures.

MINOR FESTIVALS

·8·

Survival of Judaism: Chanukah

Chanukah, probably the best-known Jewish holiday, is actually a minor festival on the Hebrew calendar. What determines whether a holiday will be designated as major or minor? Those holidays whose observance is commanded in the Torah (the first five books of the Bible) are considered major; all others are minor.

Actually, *Chanukah* is not found in the Bible at all! The story of *Chanukah* is related in the Books of the Maccabees, which are part of the Apocrypha. (The Apocrypha is a collection of religious writings, which the ancient rabbis felt were not sacred enough to be included in the Hebrew Scriptures.) The observance of *Chanukah* is also described in the Talmud.

Historical Background
Before we discuss the present-day celebration of this joyous holiday, we should give some historical background. The events commemorated by *Chanukah* took place in Judea during the second pre-Christian century, a very complex and turbulent period. At that time, Judea was part of the Syrian Empire and was heavily influenced by the Hellenistic culture that was sweeping the ancient Near East in the wake of the conquest of Alexander the Great.

The term "Hellenism" is used to refer to the spread of Greek cultural traditions in the lands that came under Greek influence. Among Jews, Hellenism was evidenced by the substitution of Greek for Hebrew and Aramaic, the use of Greek personal names, the adoption of Greek educational institutions, the growth of Jewish Hellenistic literature and philosophy, and religious deviation.

Hellenism was the first culture to transcend national boundaries and become a truly universal culture. By adopting Hellenism, it became possible, for the first time, for people to extend their world view beyond the narrow confines of their own nationality. It is not surprising, therefore, that many Jews forsook traditional Jewish study to pursue politics, philosophy, commerce, drama, and physical culture, which were all part and parcel of Hellenism. The result was a diminution of commitment to Jewish values and to the Jewish religion.

The conflict between the Jewish loyalists and the Hellenizers had political as well as religious consequences. Antiochus, the king of Syria, had attempted to unify his empire by insisting that all his subjects adopt one religion—the worship of Zeus. This religious policy offered all the people of the empire, including the Jews, the opportunity to become equals. While the Hellenizers rejoiced at this opportunity, the more traditional elements among the Jews were appalled at the idea of adopting paganism. They insisted on following the mandates of the Torah. Antiochus viewed this adherence to the Torah as an expression of nationalism that he saw as a threat to his empire. The stage was set for conflict.

Antiochus decreed that Jews abandon the Torah and Jewish practices and publicly embrace paganism. Those refusing to go along with the edict were subject to capital punishment, and, in fact, many Jews were executed.

Refusing to accept this repressive policy, a group of Jews took to the hills in order to engage in armed revolt. Led by Judah Maccabee, using guerrilla tactics against the Syrian army, the band gained control of the main road to Jerusalem. This first fight for religious freedom in human history was climaxed by the retaking of the Temple in Jerusalem, which had been desecrated by the Syrians. In an eight-day celebration, the Maccabees (as the rebels came to be known) rededicated the Temple and established an annual commemoration of this event. The holiday is called *Chanukah,* which means "dedication."

Perhaps the best-known part of the *Chanukah* story is not found in the Apocrypha at all but is related in the Talmud. There it is recounted that, when the Maccabees rededicated the Temple, they searched for oil to light the candelabrum. They could locate only one small jar of oil that should have lasted but one day, yet the candelabrum miraculously remained lit for eight days until more oil could be procured.

While some Jews today accept this talmudic account as historical fact, many others regard it simply as a lovely legend. Those who doubt its veracity ask why, if this was such a wonderful miracle, it was not included in the Books of the Maccabees. They argue that the story developed later and was included in the Talmud to emphasize God's role in the deliverance and to discourage political activism.

Since so many people associate the celebration of *Chanukah* with the account of the oil, why should people who do not accept that story celebrate *Chanukah*? There *was* a miracle at *Chanukah*, a miracle greater than that of the oil. It was the miracle of Jewish survival, the victory of the few over the many. It was a successful fight for religious freedom.

Celebrating Chanukah

How is *Chanukah* celebrated today? It is primarily a home-centered holiday, lasting for eight days beginning on the twenty-fifth day of the winter month of *Kislev* (usually around December). The central feature of its observance is the nightly lighting of the *Chanukiah*, an eight-branched candelabrum designed specifically for *Chanukah*. (There is also a place for a ninth candle, the *shamash* or *shames*, that is used to light the others.) Most people refer to the *Chanukiah* as a *menorah* though the term *menorah* is more general and can refer also to a seven-branched candelabrum.

We light the *Chanukiah* in a rather dramatic fashion. On the first night of *Chanukah*, one candle is lit; on the second night, two candles; each night an additional candle is added so that by the eighth night the *Chanukiah* is ablaze. The candles are placed in the holders from right to left but lit from left to right, thus giving first honor to the newest night of the holiday. Prior to lighting the candles, two blessings are recited or chanted: "Blessed are You, our God, Ruler of the universe, who hallows us with Your commandments and commands us to kindle the *Chanukah* lights" and "Blessed are You, our God, Ruler of the universe, who performed wondrous deeds for our ancestors in days of old, at this season." On the first night, we welcome the holiday by also reciting the *Shehecheyanu:* "Blessed are You, our God, Ruler of

Chanukah lamp; Poland, second half 18th century. From the collection of the Hebrew Union College Skirball Museum, photography by John R. Forsman.

the universe, for giving us life, for sustaining us, and for enabling us to reach this season." It is customary to sing songs immediately after lighting the *menorah*. The best known of the songs is *Maoz Tsur;* an English version of the song is entitled "Rock of Ages."

Lighting the *menorah* in this fashion symbolizes the sense of optimism that is at the core of Judaism. At the darkest season of the year when the nights are longest, we light a candle against the darkness.

Since *Chanukah* is a minor holiday, we are not expected to refrain from our normal weekly activities. However, while the candles are burning, it is customary to pause and spend time in the celebration of the holiday. Families and friends gather together for lighting the *menorah,* singing traditional *Chanukah* songs, and playing games like *dreidel*. A *dreidel* (in Hebrew, *sevivon*) is a four-sided top, with a Hebrew letter on each side. These letters, נ, ג, ה, and שׁ, are the first letters of the words in the Hebrew sentence, נם גדול היה שם (a great miracle happened there). In the *dreidel* game, each player antes up and then spins the *dreidel* in turn. If the *dreidel* lands on a נ, the player neither wins nor loses; if it lands on ג, the player wins the pot; if it lands on ה, the player wins half the pot; if it lands on ש, the player puts in an extra ante.

The ante for the *dreidel* game can take many forms. Some people use small coins (*gelt*); others use nuts, raisins, or candies. Many families give *Chanukah gelt* (money) to their children as a *Chanukah* gift. From this practice developed more elaborate gift-giving (partly in response to a feeling of having to compete with Christmas).

The *dreidel* game is often part of a *Chanukah* party. The most commonly served food at such parties is potato *latkes* (potato pancakes). In Hebrew, they are known as *levivot*. Also gaining in popularity are *sufganiot* (jelly donuts). These types of foods are served because they are fried in oil, reminding us of the legend of the oil that lasted for eight days.

A Minority in a Majority Culture: Jews and Christmas

At this time of the year, Jews are especially conscious of being members of a minority. Often, it seems as though the whole world were celebrating Christmas. Christmas decorations go up in stores and on streets a month or more before the holiday; carols pour forth from the radio and the local shopping mall. Children are urged to visit Santa Claus.

How are Jews to respond to all this? The first thing we must do is come to terms with what Christmas is. While it is true that, to some extent, Christmas has become secularized, at root it remains a major religious festival of Christianity. There are people who believe that God looked at this world and decided that the only way to solve its problems was to come to earth in human form. And, for those people, Christmas marks the event when God took on human form. There is a name for people who hold this belief—"Christian." If you accept this teaching, the holiday is yours; if you don't, it is not.

Some people are concerned that their children will feel deprived if they do not celebrate Christmas. Actually, children are willing to accept that different people celebrate different holidays. For instance, from a very young age, children go to birthday parties. They know that they are there to celebrate someone else's birthday and are not upset when the birthday child receives presents and the guests do not.

There are people who would argue that Christmas has become secular. They do not believe in Christian doctrines, but they enjoy the warm feelings and the beauty associated with the season. They argue that the Christmas tree is not really a Christian symbol and that the spirit of Christmas is universal. To those people we would ask: Do non-Christians have the right to trivialize one of the most sacred and most important days of the Christian year?

Does this mean that Jews should have nothing at all to do with Christmas? We live in a largely Christian environment, and certainly it is appropriate to wish our Christian friends well on their holiday, send them gifts, visit their homes, help them decorate their Christmas trees, and attend their Christmas parties. All these can be done as long as there is the recognition that Christmas is *their* special day, not ours.

Since the days of the Maccabees, living as a minority in the midst of a majority culture and maintaining our identity and our integrity has not always been easy. Choosing to live a Jewish life often requires dedication and devotion. The theme of *Chanukah* is that the few can exist with the many—that a people small in number can survive and flourish. This should be an inspiration to all Jews.

·9·

Survival of the
Jewish People: Purim

One of the merriest days of the Jewish year is the early spring holiday of *Purim*. The source of the holiday is the biblical Book of Esther.

The Story of Purim

The story takes place in Persia during the reign of King Ahasuerus. The king orders Vashti, his wife, to appear at one of the banquets he was accustomed to giving. When she refuses (an early martyr to women's liberation?), the king, enraged, gets rid of her. The most beautiful maidens in the kingdom are called to the capital so that Ahasuerus may choose a new queen. Among these beautiful maidens is Esther, whose guardian, Mordecai, has instructed her not to reveal her Jewish origins. The king chooses her as his new queen because of her beauty and special charms, and Mordecai is appointed to a position as guardian in the King's Gate. In this way, Mordecai can be in a position to know how Esther is faring.

One day, Mordecai overhears two of King Ahasuerus's courtiers plotting to assassinate the king. Mordecai reports the plot, and the conspirators are executed. The incident is noted in the court chronicles but is then forgotten. Meanwhile, the king has named Haman to be his chief minister. Mordecai refuses to bow down to Haman, enraging the arrogant chief minister, who decides to take revenge upon Mordecai and his entire people. Haman goes to the king and accuses the Jews of disloyalty to the king, citing the fact that they are "different" as an example of that disloyalty. Haman gets permission from the king to destroy the entire people on one day. By the casting of lots (*purim*), the thirteenth day of *Adar* is chosen as the day of the massacre, and messengers are sent throughout the kingdom to prepare the mobs for the massacre.

Esther, who is in the women's quarters, is completely unaware of this plot. Mordecai sends word to her to intercede with the king on behalf of her people. After some vacillation because of the extreme danger in appearing before the king unbidden, Esther fasts for three days and then goes to the king. Ahasuerus receives her with favor. She invites him and Haman to a feast. Haman is delighted, interpreting this invitation as a sign of royal favor. After preparing a gallows for Mordecai, Haman goes to the banquet. Esther then invites the king and Haman to another banquet on the following day.

That night, the king, unable to sleep, asks that the royal chronicles be read to him. He hears of Mordecai's denunciation of the plotters and learns that Mordecai never received a reward. The king asks Haman what should be done for one whom the king wishes to honor. Haman, assuming that the king means to honor him, responds with a list of lavish gifts and honors. The king, pleased with the response, orders Haman to arrange these honors for Mordecai. Haman, though chagrined, must obey.

That night he goes to the second banquet with Esther and the king. The king asks Esther what she would like from him, and she pleads for her life and the lives of her people. Ahasuerus, of course, is unaware that his beloved queen was among those who were to be executed. When Esther names Haman as the villain, Haman and his ten sons are hanged upon the gallows that he had had erected for Mordecai.

Mordecai now is elevated to Haman's former position of chief minister. However, the decree, once issued, cannot be rescinded. Mordecai suggests that another decree be issued, enabling the Jews to resist any who might rise up against them because of the first decree.

On the thirteenth of *Adar*, mobs rose up against the Jews but were repulsed by them. The Jews celebrated their deliverance with a festival on the fourteenth of *Adar*, observed by giving gifts to the poor, exchanging gifts with one another, and rejoicing. The biblical book ends with

Esther case scroll; Eastern Europe, early 19th century. From the collection of the Hebrew Union College Skirball Museum, photography by John R. Forsman.

Mordecai and Esther calling upon Jews everywhere to observe *Purim* as a perpetual holiday.

The Megillah

The *Megillah* of Esther almost sounds like the plot of an opera. Did the events in this story actually take place? Scholars disagree as to the historicity of the tale. While we can never know for certain, it is undeniably true that the Book of Esther delivers an important message that transcends the questions of whether and when the story "really" happened. It is a message of survival and courage and the *human* capacity to change history. (This is the only book of the Bible in which God is never mentioned.)

This story celebrates Jewish survival, and Jews, on the fourteenth of *Adar,* celebrate *Purim.* We are obligated to hear the story, to hear "the *Megillah*," as the Book of Esther is commonly known. As we have noted in Chapter 4, there are actually five *megillot* (scrolls) that are read on five different holidays: the Book of Esther is read on *Purim;* the Song of Songs is read on Passover; the Book of Ruth is read on *Shavuot;* Lamentations is read on the Ninth Day of *Av;* and Ecclesiastes is read on *Sukot.* These scrolls are somewhat different in appearance from the Torah scrolls in the synagogue in that they have only one roller.

The Book of Esther is read during special *Purim* services that are marked by great revelry. Each time Haman's name is read, we are obligated to drown it out by making as much noise as is humanly possible. Most people use *groggers,* special *Purim* noisemakers, but it

Purim grogger; U.S.A., 20th century. From the collection of the Hebrew Union College Skirball Museum, photography by Lelo Carter.

is also permissible to use any other noisemakers. Haman's name can be drowned out as well by whistling, cat-calling, hissing, booing, stomping, or by whatever means are at one's disposal. It is customary for young and old alike to come to services in costume.

Purim in the Synagogue

Many congregations stage *Purimspiels,* special and very humorous plays that are a *Purim* tradition. During the *Purimspiel,* anything goes—the sillier the better. *Purimspiels* are one example of Jewish humor—a brand of humor growing out of the Jewish experience, which was often harsh. In order to survive, it was necessary to learn how to laugh at certain difficult conditions—and at ourselves as well. Jewish humor is often marked by an element of irony. Following are a few Yiddish proverbs that give the flavor:

> It's a good idea to send a lazy
> person for the Angel of Death.

> A boil is fine, as long as it's
> under someone else's arm.

> If a fool holds the cow by the
> horns, a clever person can milk
> her.

In addition to *Purim* services and *Purimspiels,* many synagogues have *Purim* parades and *Purim* carnivals. Drinking to excess is also a *Purim* tradition. In fact, traditionally, we are supposed to drink so much that we can no longer distinguish between the words "Blessed be Mordecai" and "Cursed be Haman." (Of course, drivers are exempt from strict observance of this custom!)

Customs and Observance

Even though this is a holiday marked by joyous excess, it is also marked by the giving of *tsedakah* (to at least two needy persons) and the giving of gifts of food to friends (*mishlo'ach manot*) as mentioned in Esther 9:19, 22. *Mishlo'ach manot* (also known as *shalach monos*) generally consists of plates or baskets of *hamantashen* (filled three-cornered pastries supposed to represent Haman's hat), fruits and nuts, or candies. The tradition is to give at least two ready-to-eat foods.

Some Jews have a *seudah* (feast) on *Purim* afternoon. This is a perfect opportunity to extend hospitality.

While *Purim* is one of our very happiest holidays, it does have a serious underlying theme—anti-Semitism—that is often discussed on *Shabbat Zachor,* the *Shabbat* that precedes *Purim.*

Anti-Semitism

Haman is seen as a prototype for the anti-Semite. His message was that the Jews are different and, therefore, must be destroyed. Since Haman, unfortunately, there have been numerous instances of government-sanctioned anti-Semitism. In recent history alone we have seen Czarist *pogroms,* the Nazi war against the Jews, and Soviet repression of *refuseniks* (those Jews who have been refused exit visas from the Soviet Union). And then there is the matter of "polite" anti-Semitism: quotas in school admissions, restricted neighborhoods, discrimination in employment.

But, although Jewish life has not always been easy, still we rejoice in our survival—in the fact that we have endured and thrived—and on *Purim* we celebrate our survival and our capacity to influence history.

NEW FESTIVALS

·10·

A World Destroyed:
Yom Hashoah

The Holocaust has seared itself into the consciousness of Jews, and after more than forty years its impact is felt even more keenly. Hardly a month goes by that doesn't mark the appearance of a book or film or study on the impact of this bleak chapter in human history. Before World War II, approximately 8,700,000 Jews lived in Europe. By war's end, some 6,000,000 of them had been murdered. That is the end of the story, but where does it begin?

The World of Eastern Europe

From the Middle Ages Jews lived in Eastern Europe, sometimes in cities but more often in small communities (*shtetlach;* singular, *shtetl*) where they had highly developed community institutions. Yiddish was the everyday language; Hebrew was considered a holy language, to be used only in the sacred texts and for prayers. Yiddish is a form of medieval German, with loan words from Hebrew as well as many other languages, and is written in Hebrew characters. It is known affectionately as *mamaloshen,* the mother tongue. However, Yiddish was not only an everyday language. It gave rise to a rich literary and theatrical tradition. This literature has been enriched in the nineteenth and twentieth centuries by such luminaries as Sholom Aleichem, I. L. Peretz, and Isaac Bashevis Singer. In addition, Eastern European Jews had the opportunity to be exposed to the classics of Western literature since many of them were translated into Yiddish.

The world of the *shtetl* is often idealized by modern Jews. It was not a perfect place by any means. *Shtetl* Jews were often poor and were restricted as to where they could live and what occupations they could follow. They were not all one hundred percent pious, but many were fervently religious. The *shtetl* was not immune to the winds of change that swept through nineteenth-century Eastern Europe. The Enlightenment (Western secular intellectual knowledge of philosophy and literature) was a threat to the cohesiveness of the Jewish community. *Pogroms* (organized attacks on the Jewish community) were a constant danger.

The Eastern European *shtetl* exists only in memory and in artifacts. It was the origin of the majority of American Jews whose grandparents arrived in the great waves of immigration around the turn of the century. Although there are still some Jews living in Eastern Europe, the rich and vital world of Eastern European Jewry perished in the Holocaust.

Anti-Semitism

The Holocaust came about largely as a result of a climate of anti-Semitism that had pervaded European culture for many hundreds of years. Anti-Semitism, the irrational hatred of Jews, can be traced back to at least New Testament times. For instance, in the eighth chapter of the Gospel of John we find: "You [Jews] are of your father the devil, and your will is to do your father's desires," and "he who is of God hears the words of God; the reason why you do not hear them is that you are not of God." (*The Holy Bible. Revised Standard Version Bible,* 1971) Newly developing Christian theology took on the thrust that, because the Jews rejected Jesus, God had rejected the Jews and shifted favor to the Church, which came to see itself as the New Israel. Therefore, any ill that befell the Jews was God's punishment, brought upon themselves by stubbornly and blindly refusing to accept Jesus as their Savior. At the beginning of the third century, Origen, one of the fathers of the early Church, stated: "We may thus assert in utter confidence that the Jews will not return to their earlier situation, for they have committed the most abominable of crimes, in forming this conspiracy against the Savior of the human race. . . . Hence the city where Jesus suffered was necessarily destroyed, the Jewish nation was driven from its country, and another people was called by God to the blessed election." (Leon Poliakov, *The History of Anti-Semitism*. New York: Schocken, 1965, p. 23)

The fourth-century preacher Gregory of Nyssa described Jews as "murderers of the Lord, assassins of the prophets, rebels, and detestors of God, they outraged the Law, resist grace, repudiate the faith of their fathers. Companions of the devil, race of vipers, informers, calumniators, darkeners of the mind, pharisaic leaven, Sanhedrin of demons, accursed, detested, lapidators, enemies of all that is beautiful. . . ." (Poliakov, *The History of Anti-Semitism*, p. 25)

The view of Jews as demons was expressed most forcefully by the fourth-century Church father St. John Chrysostom: "The synagogue is not only a place of vice and impiety. It is a haunt of the demons. The very souls of Jews are haunts of demons." (Rosemary Radford Ruether, *Faith and Fratricide*. New York: Seabury Press, 1974, p. 178) While Chrysostom did not order his followers to attack Jews, the implication of his words was rather clear: "When animals are unfit for work, they are marked for slaughter, and this is the very thing which the Jews have experienced. By making themselves unfit for work, they have become ready for slaughter. This is why Christ said: 'Ask for my enemies, who did not want me to reign over them, bring them here, and slay them before me.' " (Ruether, *Faith and Fratricide*, p. 179)

This pattern of hatred, established early on by the Church fathers, continued throughout the ensuing centuries. During the Crusades, for instance, on their way to liberate the Holy Land from the "infidels," the Crusaders realized that they had "infidels" in their midst, namely Jews living in villages on the routes leading to the Holy Land. So they began their Crusade by indiscriminately plundering, torturing, raping, and murdering thousands of Jews.

Anti-Jewish feeling was seen again in the activities of the Church Office of the Inquisition. Under Church influence, King Ferdinand of Spain expelled all Jews from his realm in 1492. While many Jews left the country, others chose to remain and converted to do so. Some of these converts secretly practiced Judaism and came to be known pejoratively as Marranos, a word meaning "swine" in Spanish. In order to root out Jewish belief, the Inquisition employed the most brutal forms of torture. In many cases, people of Jewish background from families that had been believing and practicing Catholics for generations were arrested and tortured until they "admitted" to being secret Jews. They were then burned at the stake, and their property was confiscated.

Throughout the centuries, anti-Semites manufactured a number of calumnies to arouse hostility against the Jews on the part of the populace. One of these was the "blood libel," according to which Jews were accused of kidnapping and murdering Christian children in order to use their blood for the baking of *matzah*. Another accusation was that of the desecration of the Host. The anti-Semites claimed that Jews would sneak into a church at night, steal consecrated communion wafers (the consecrated communion wafer, according to Catholic teaching, is the body of Christ), and desecrate them. Yet another false charge was that Jews poisoned the wells from which Christians drank. These accusations stirred up mobs of frenzied fanatics and moved them to violent physical attacks on Jews. Such attacks, known in Russia as *pogroms,* were often instigated by government officials and abetted by church leaders.

The Holocaust

Centuries of anti-Jewish teachings created fertile ground for the seed of Nazi hatred to flourish. The people had been conditioned to despise Jews and to see them as something less than human. Thus they could rationalize the elimination of the Jews, not as murder, but as the removal of a cancerous element in society or the destruction of parasites or vermin.

Millions of people from many ethnic backgrounds were killed in Nazi extermination camps, but Adolf Hitler single-mindedly pursued with ferocious intensity his goal of destroying the Jewish people. He conceived of it as "the final solution of the Jewish problem." The beastly destruction of some six million Jews (including one and a half million children) is well documented and need not be elaborated here. The names of Auschwitz, Bergen-Belsen, Dachau, and many more camps remain emblazoned in the memory of the generation that witnessed the atrocities and those who have learned of it since. The elimination of over six million individual human beings solely because they were Jews is its own kind of horror.

Jewish Resistance

One often hears the question raised: "Why did they go like sheep to the slaughter?" The question implies a perception that is inaccurate. The fact is there was a good deal of resistance, both physical and spiritual.

Perhaps the best known act of resistance was the Warsaw Ghetto

Uprising. Mightily outnumbered, woefully underequipped, with no military experience or expertise and no real history of combat, Jews in the Warsaw Ghetto, under the leadership of Mordecai Anielewicz, made a valiant stand that constituted the largest battle in occupied Europe up to that time (except in Yugoslavia). On April 19, 1943, a German force of tanks and artillery entered the ghetto and attempted to resume deportation of Jews to concentration camps. They met stiff resistance, were repulsed, and suffered numerous casualties. They tried again, and again fought several days, encountering resistance. It was only when they began to burn the ghetto house by house (with the inhabitants inside) that they began to get the upper hand. Even so, the Jews continued fighting fiercely. Their headquarters fell on May 8, but resistance continued until June. Even after the ghetto fell, those Jews that had escaped to the forest and those hidden in the ghetto continued to resist.

Many nameless Jews were moved to acts of heroism during this period. The memory of others, whose names are known, lives on as a blessing. Among these is Hannah Senesh, a brave young woman who had managed to escape from Europe to Palestine, and who then, after volunteering to return and be parachuted behind enemy lines, was caught and killed. Another hero was Janusz Korczak, a highly respected physician and educator, who directed the Jewish orphanage in Warsaw. During the Nazi deportation of the ghetto, the Germans offered him his freedom, but he refused to abandon his charges and chose instead to accompany them to Treblinka where both they and he perished. Leo Baeck was a great rabbinic scholar and leader of German Jewry who even in the Theresienstadt concentration camp continued to teach and provide spiritual resistance for the people.

In spite of the many instances of resistance, we might still ask: "Why did any Jews go to their deaths without a fight?" The question implies a perspective that people in the midst of a situation could not be expected to have. It is important to remember that throughout much of Jewish history Jews had been a powerless minority, faced with constant harassment but never total annihilation. Jews learned to survive by keeping a low profile and waiting things out. In this case, the approach that had always worked turned out to be disastrous. The people were psychologically demoralized, hungry, and physically exhausted. Furthermore, people always believe that "it can't happen here." Often, by the time the Jews realized what was really happening, it was simply too late.

Not all resistance is physical. Much of the resistance that did occur might be termed spiritual. In spite of the humiliation and degradation, for one to maintain a measure of dignity and humanity in those times was to resist. For instance, the ghettos and concentration camps were squalid, miserable places where the people were forced to live in less-than-human conditions. Nevertheless, the Jews kept their spirits alive by organizing classes, lectures, musical events, and religious observances.

While all the details making up the enormity of the Holocaust were not known as they were occurring, as the war progressed more and more information became public. Why didn't the rest of the world intervene? Partly because people were skeptical of war atrocity stories. Partly because all energies were being devoted to winning the war in the battlefield. Partly because of apathy. Partly because it was "only" the Jews.

Righteous Gentiles

A notable exception to the worldwide apathy was the courageous action of Denmark and Sweden. Denmark had been occupied by the Nazis who planned to deport the Jews to concentration camps. The Danes decided to save their Jews and organized a secret evacuation by ferry to neighboring Sweden, which was neutral and willing to accept the entire Jewish population of Denmark.

While most nations may not have acted, individuals did. There were many Righteous Gentiles that risked their lives to save Jews. They hid Jews in their homes, smuggled food to Jews, forged passports, and assisted in numerous other ways. Many who were caught paid for their courage with their lives.

One of the ways the world Jewish community has honored these Righteous Gentiles is by planting, at *Yad Vashem,* a row of trees, each one bearing the name of a person known to have saved Jewish lives. Visitors who come to this central Holocaust memorial, located in Jerusalem, must approach it by walking along a path lined by these trees. *Yad Vashem,* like Holocaust memorials throughout the world, stands as a reminder of the destruction of European Jewry. Those who are no more can live on only in memory; by remembering them we affirm life and continuity.

Contemporary Remembrance of the Holocaust

The children of the Holocaust survivors have now reached adulthood. This second generation has joined together to promote awareness and memory of the Holocaust.

Many synagogues include in their *Yom Kippur* services special readings relating to the Holocaust. One addition to the Passover *seder* is the inclusion of readings recalling the Holocaust. Also, some congregations, as part of the regular *Shabbat* services, mention the victims of the Holocaust before the recitation of *Kaddish*.

A special Holocaust Memorial Day, called *Yom Hashoah,* has been set aside for annual observance each year. It occurs on the twenty-seventh day of *Nisan*. Many temples hold special services for *Yom Hashoah,* and most larger Jewish communities conduct a citywide commemorative program. Many Jews whose relatives died in the concentration camps observe *Yom Hashoah* as the *yahrzeit* for those relatives because their exact date of death is unknown.

Jews are often challenged: "Why can't you just forget the Holocaust? Why do you keep bringing it up?" We can't forget it because it was our family that was murdered. Jews throughout the world feel related to one another and feel that we are part of a large extended family. At the same time Jews recognize that we represent only a tiny fraction of the world's population (about thirteen million Jews out of a total world population of about five billion, which is approximately one-quarter of one percent).

However, we bring up the Holocaust not simply because it is a *Jewish* tragedy. We talk about it because we believe that the world must not be allowed to forget it. Twelve million innocent human beings, six million of them Jews, were murdered by the Nazis. The lesson of the Holocaust is that a crime of such proportions must never be allowed to happen again. We keep the memory of the Holocaust before the world as a way of guarding against the wanton destruction of any people.

·11·

Zionism and the State of Israel: Yom Ha'atsmaut

While the State of Israel formally declared its independence in May 1948, the history of Israel began long before. Wherever Jews have lived, and in whatever time, they have always felt a strong emotional bond with the land of Israel. This tie between land and people goes back to Abraham, the very first Jew, whose descendants were promised the land as an inheritance. (Genesis 12:7) During most of the biblical period, the Jews lived in the land. Even after the destruction of the Temple in Jerusalem in the year 70, when the majority of the Jews were dispersed throughout the world, there remained the hope that someday they would be able to return to live in the land of their ancestors. This hope was never lost and is reflected in Jewish liturgy and literature.

While there has always been a Jewish presence in the land of Israel since the year 70, it was only from the nineteenth century onward that Jews in any significant number came to settle the land once more.

In 1881–82 Russian Jewry experienced a series of *pogroms* in which hundreds of Jews were murdered, many Jewish women raped, and Jewish villages looted and destroyed. Jews were very vulnerable, and in this climate of persecution many of them left Russia. The largest group went to America and other Western countries while a small number went to what was then known as Palestine and is now Israel.

An incident in 1895 in France transformed the ages-old longing of

Jews for a homeland into a movement, Zionism—a movement that would result ultimately in the establishment of a Jewish state. Captain Alfred Dreyfus, a Jewish officer in the French army, was falsely accused of betraying France to Germany. Crowds gathered screaming "Death to the Jews!" It was because of this display of anti-Semitism that Dreyfus was convicted on fabricated evidence and sentenced to life imprisonment on Devil's Island. (He later was exonerated.)

The Dreyfus trial made a lasting impact on Theodor Herzl, a Jewish journalist who reported on it for a leading Viennese newspaper. Like many assimilated Jews, Herzl had believed that the persecution of Jews throughout history was coming to an end as a result of the advances made by humanity in the modern age. Witnessing this horrifying display of mob emotion against the backdrop of Paris, one of the world's most elegant and civilized cities, he was convinced that Jews had no real, positive future in Europe. The next year, his book, *The Jewish State: An Attempt at a Modern Solution to the Jewish Question,* appeared. In it, Herzl stated that Jews could escape the dangers of modern anti-Semitism only by creating their own state.

Zionism

In 1897, Herzl gathered representatives from Jewish communities around the world, who were interested in taking action in pursuit of the dream. After this First Zionist Congress, Herzl wrote in his diary: "At Basle, I created the Jewish state."

The creation of a Jewish state is what Zionism was all about. Zionism is the belief that there should be a Jewish homeland in Zion. What is Zion? Zion is actually a place name. It is a mountain in Jerusalem. It came to mean the entire city of Jerusalem and, by extension, the whole land of Israel. The term "Zion" ultimately came to express the yearning of the Jewish people for their homeland.

The pursuit of the Zionist dream proceeded along two tracks: the political and the economic. In the political sphere, Zionist representatives sought to gain support for a Jewish homeland from world leaders. In the economic sphere, the early Zionists, realizing that they had to acquire the land, began actively to raise funds that would enable them to purchase the land from the absentee Turkish landlords. The agency for accomplishing this task was the Jewish National Fund. Individuals made contributions to the JNF, and the JNF, in turn, purchased property on behalf

The Emek; Israel, c. 1920. From the collection of the Hebrew Union College Skirball Museum, photography by S. J. Schweig.

Jerusalem; Israel, 1980. Photography by Bill Aron.

of the Jewish people as a whole. The JNF was the purchasing instrumentality of the collective known as the Jewish people.

The program strongly captured the imagination of Jews everywhere. Soon, in many Jewish homes, the JNF "blue box" appeared. By placing coins in this small, tin donation can (*pushke*), the average Jew was able to become an active participant in the realization of the dream—the resettlement of the Jewish people on its own land.

Zionism was more than a political movement; it had a cultural facet as well. Zionism led to the rebirth of the Hebrew language. In the postbiblical era prior to modern times, Hebrew was used solely for prayer and study of sacred texts. As Jews began to settle the land in sizable numbers, Hebrew became the spoken language, with many new words being coined to bring the language into the twentieth century. The man most responsible for modernizing the language was Eliezer ben Yehuda. The cultural facet of Zionism was not limited to language; there was also a flowering of Hebrew literature. The great spokesman for cultural Zionism was the essayist who wrote under the pen name Ahad Ha-Am.

While we have touched on the political, economic, and cultural aspects of Zionism separately, in fact they were developing simultaneously. Thus cultural, economic, and political growth was taking place in the Jewish homeland. In 1917, international recognition of this growth was given in the form of the Balfour Declaration. In that document, the British government acknowledged the right of the Jewish people to a homeland in Palestine. This was particularly significant because, at the end of World War I, Great Britain was given the mandate by the League of Nations to govern Palestine.

Establishment of the Modern State of Israel

The road to independence was not a smooth one. This was an era of emerging nationalism, and what resulted in the Middle East was a clash of Jewish nationalism and Arab nationalism. This clash manifested itself in a series of murderous attacks on Jews.

In 1922, the British separated that part of Palestine that was east of the Jordan River, thus creating the Arab state of Transjordan. In the ensuing years, the Arabs influenced the British to restrict severely Jewish immigration to Palestine. This policy became especially heartbreaking for the Jews during the Nazi era. Thousands of Jews fleeing from Nazi-occupied Europe were sent back to their certain death because there was no place of refuge for them. By 1947, conflicts between Jews and Arabs had steadily escalated to the point where the British chose to withdraw. The United Nations voted to partition the territory into a Jewish section and an Arab section. In May 1948, when the British did withdraw, the Jews declared the Jewish section of the territory an independent state, naming it Israel. A 1,900-year-old dream had become reality.

While independence had been achieved, peace had not. All of the Arab countries joined forces and attacked Israel. By 1949, an armistice was reached. While it meant the cessation of warfare, it did not signify peace.

In the early years of statehood, under the leadership of David Ben-Gurion, Israel absorbed hundreds of thousands of Jewish immigrants— the displaced persons of the concentration camps as well as those from Arab lands who had come to feel unwelcome in their native lands. At the same time, the Arabs that chose to leave Israel at the time it declared independence were not integrated into the Arab lands where they now found themselves. Instead, most of them were placed and kept in refugee camps, where resentment of and hatred for Israel have been fomented from that time until the present.

The position of the Arab states has been that Israel does not have the right to exist. In 1967, Egypt, Syria, and Jordan joined together in an attempt to destroy Israel. That effort was ended six days later with a smashing Israeli victory, one result of which was the reuniting of Jerusalem, which had been divided during the War of Independence. In 1973, once again Israel was attacked, this time by Egypt and Syria. Again, Israel was victorious. Since that time, only Egypt has chosen to sign a peace treaty with Israel. All the other Arab nations are, technically, still at war with Israel.

Relationship of Diaspora Jews to Israel

One cannot overestimate the depth of feeling that Diaspora Jews (living outside Israel) have for Israel. Jews everywhere understand that Israel is the one place in the world where Jews are always welcome. Israel has had a strong impact on Diaspora Jewish life. Israeli songs, dances, and foods have become popular. The study of modern Hebrew has become widespread.

Israel and the Diaspora are interdependent. The Diaspora communities lend moral, political, and financial support to our fellow Jews in

Israel. The largest amount of financial support for social welfare and educational services is channeled through the United Jewish Appeal. In return, we derive inspiration. Although there is unqualified support for Israel's right to exist and devotion to Israel's well-being, this does not mean that American Jews automatically agree with every Israeli government policy. Issues involving Israel are often the topic of lively debate by Jews outside of Israel. However, the underlying support for Israel remains firm.

The anniversary of Israel's declaration of independence is celebrated annually on the fifth of *Iyar* (corresponding to April or early May). This holiday, known as *Yom Ha'atsmaut*, is marked by parades and fireworks in Israel. Many Diaspora communities observe it as well, often with special services, programs, and marches.

Jews today are privileged to live in a time in which the impossible became possible. For many Jews, the existence of the State of Israel is nothing less than a miracle.

The Cycle of Life

◆ ◆ ◆

ENTERING THE COVENANT

CREATING A HOME

TRANSITION

ENTERING THE COVENANT

· 12 ·

Forging a Link in the Chain: Birth

In Judaism, family is central. The synagogue is certainly an important institution, but, since so many of our observances occur within the family setting, we may fairly say that the home is the center of Jewish life. Indeed, the home is referred to as *mikdash me'at,* a small sanctuary.

"Be Fruitful and Multiply"

Much of our family life revolves around our children. The first human couple was blessed in these words: "Be fruitful and multiply, fill the earth and master it." (Genesis 1:28) So procreation is seen as both a *mitzvah* (a religious observance) and a blessing.

Each person experiences peak periods in life, such as birth, puberty, marriage, and death. Every culture marks these periods with special ceremonies, "rites of passage." Judaism has developed many customs that invest these moments with transcendent meaning.

Anyone who has witnessed the birth of a child knows the exaltation of that experience. Every birth is a miracle in which we can sense the presence of the Divine. Jews welcome God's gift of a new life with ceremony, by entering that child into the covenant.

Berit

The covenant, called *berit* in Hebrew, is the sacred agreement between God and Abraham. It is a pact of loyalty between us—Abraham's descendants—and our God. Circumcision is a sign of that covenant, as prescribed in Genesis 17:9–12: "God further said to Abraham, 'As for you, you and your offspring to come throughout the ages shall keep My covenant. Such shall be the covenant between Me and you and your offspring to follow which you shall keep: every male among you shall be circumcised. You shall circumcise the flesh of your foreskin, and that shall be the sign of the covenant between Me and you. And throughout the generations, every male among you shall be circumcised at the age of eight days.' "

Thus, for Jews, circumcision is not merely a hygienic operation; it is a deeply religious and significant event. The ceremony surrounding the circumcision is called *Berit Milah,* the Covenant of Circumcision (commonly referred to as *berit* or *b'ris*). Unless the child's health forces a postponement, it is held on the eighth day of a boy's life. The circumcision itself is traditionally performed by a *mohel,* a highly trained ritual circumciser. Orthodox, most Conservative, and many Reform Jews have a *mohel* officiate at their son's circumcision. Some Reform Jews will have a physician perform the circumcision and a rabbi conduct the ceremony of *Berit Milah,* which usually takes place at home, or occasionally in the synagogue or at the hospital. The Reform movement has a training program for physicians who wish to become *mohalim.*

It is customary to have candles lit at the *Berit Milah* ceremony. A chair is set aside in honor of the prophet Elijah. A blessing is made over wine, a taste of which is given to the baby. A Hebrew name is bestowed upon the little boy, along with a prayer that he will be blessed with a life of Torah study, marital bliss, and days filled with good deeds. Relatives or friends are often honored at the ceremony: Those who carry the baby into the *berit* ceremony are known as the *kvatter* (godfather) and *kvatterin* (godmother), and the person who holds the baby during the ceremony is called the *sandak.* At the conclusion of the *b'ris* it is traditional to have a *seudat mitzvah,* a festive meal honoring the observance of a *mitzvah.*

In Orthodox tradition, there is no *berit* ceremony for girls. Instead, it is customary for the father (or grandfather) to be called to the Torah during synagogue services and for a special prayer to be offered for the newborn. The prayer begins with the words *Mi sheberach* (May the One who blessed); within this prayer the little girl's Hebrew name is mentioned, and in this way she is formally named.

In Reform temples, the common practice has been for the naming

Circumcision bench (the chair of Elijah); Westphalia, Germany, 1803. From the collection of the Hebrew Union College Skirball Museum, photography by John R. Forsman.

of girls to take place at a Friday evening service when both mother and father are present. In recent years, some people have chosen to have a more elaborate naming ceremony for their daughters at home. This ceremony is called *Berit Hachayim,* the Covenant of Life, or *Berit Habat,* the Covenant for a (newborn) Daughter.

It is the custom among Jews stemming from Central or Eastern Europe (*Ashkenazim*) to name children after the deceased. Jews whose origin is in the Mediterranean basin (*Sephardim*) generally name children in honor of the living (often, grandparents). American Jews, depending upon their backgrounds, will follow Ashkenazic or Sephardic practice when choosing their child's Hebrew name. They will often select an English name that begins with the same letter or sound as the Hebrew name.

Other Ceremonies and Customs

There are a number of folk customs surrounding the birth of a baby: tying a red ribbon on the crib, not having a baby shower prior to the birth, and not telling the name of the child until the naming ceremony, among others. Many of these customs are related to a folk belief in the "evil eye" and are a means of averting its malevolent power.

According to folk belief, any good fortune brought with it the risk of attracting the "evil eye." One often hears the Yiddish expression *kinna hurra*. It is a form of the phrase *Ken ayin hara* (May there be no evil eye), and it is used whenever something good happens. Folk beliefs are a matter of custom and not religious law. However, they are often preserved with tenacity, and people are reluctant to give them up.

Pidyon Haben means "redemption of the (firstborn) son." It is a ceremony dating back to biblical times. A mother's firstborn child, if a male, was committed to service in the Temple in Jerusalem. By paying five *shekels* to a *kohen* (a priest—a descendant of Aaron) on the thirty-first day of the boy's life, his father redeemed the child from this obligation. In recent years, some parents whose firstborn child is a girl have developed a parallel ceremony called *Pidyon Habat*.

Many Reform Jews are uncomfortable with the concept of redemption from priestly service that underlies the *Pidyon Haben* ceremony. They either have no ceremony or opt for a newly developed ceremony, *Kiddush Pe'ter Rechem* (Sanctification of the Opening of the Womb), that celebrates the birth of a first child. Instead of giving money to a *kohen,* it is given to *tsedakah.*

Relationship between Parents and Children

The relationship between parents and children is based not only on love but also on mutual responsibility. The Talmud speaks about parents' obligations toward their children. Parents must give their children a system of values to live by, the education requisite to making a living, and basic survival skills such as swimming, thus preparing them to take their places in the world as responsible adults.

In turn, the Bible commands children to honor and respect their parents. The Talmud makes these attitudes concrete when it states that children should not contradict their parents and children must see to the physical comfort of their parents. Intergenerational responsibility and devotion have certainly been the hallmarks of Jewish life through the centuries.

Adoption

Many families are enriched through the adoption of children. While there is no formal adoption ceremony in Judaism, several beautiful prayers have been written for the adoption of a child and a grandchild. These may be found on pages 109–110 of *Gates of the House* (the Reform prayer book with devotions and ceremonies for the home, edited by Chaim Stern and published by the Central Conference of American Rabbis in 1976). The question is often raised as to whether an adopted child must be converted to Judaism. According to Jewish law, children born to a non-Jewish mother do have to be converted. Many Reform rabbis would regard such children as Jewish without conversion if the parents reared and educated them as Jews.

Birth Control

Since Judaism places such a high value on children, how does it view contraception? Within Orthodox Judaism, there is a somewhat restrictive attitude toward birth control. Some Orthodox authorities do not permit any form of birth control. Other scholars allow for the postponement of the fulfillment of the *mitzvah* of procreation, but they insist that the means of contraception must not interfere with the woman's sexual pleasure and, therefore, they limit the means of contraception.

The Reform position is that the right of parents to determine the size of their family should be respected. While the practice of birth control is approved, couples are urged to give serious consideration to the problem of Jewish survival as they deliberate their own family size.

Abortion

The topic of abortion has been much debated in recent years. While Judaism insists upon the sanctity of human life, feticide is not considered to be homicide. The Talmud clearly states that, when the continuation of a pregnancy threatens a woman's life, that pregnancy must be terminated. Thus Orthodox Judaism permits therapeutic abortions. Nontherapeutic abortions generally are not countenanced. However, in the case of pregnancy resulting from rape or incest an abortion is allowed, and in the situation of a potentially deformed child there is a tendency toward leniency. The Reform view is that the preservation of a woman's emotional health is as important as that of her physical well-being, and, therefore, nontherapeutic abortions may be considered. Because we are dealing with potential life, abortion should not be undertaken lightly and certainly should not be viewed as an alternative to contraception.

Parenthood is a privilege, a responsibility, and a blessing. A portion of our immortality is achieved through our children. Children can bring light, joy, and satisfaction to our lives. The birth of a child is an exalted moment, celebrated with thanksgiving to God by parents, relatives, friends, and the community at large.

·13·

Choosing Judaism:
Conversion

A story is told in the Talmud of a non-Jew who approached the great sage Shammai and offered to convert to Judaism if Shammai could teach him all of Judaism while he, the questioner, stood on one foot. Shammai, feeling that he—and perhaps his religion—were being mocked, angrily chased the questioner away. The man then approached the other outstanding scholar of the generation, Hillel, and made the same request. Hillel responded: "What is hurtful to you, do not do to others. That is the whole Torah. The rest is commentary. Now go and study."

What do we learn from this story? We learn, first of all, that in every age there have been those who, though not born Jewish, have sought to become part of the Jewish people. We learn that study is an important component in the process of choosing Judaism. We learn, too, that we are to meet with seriousness and with openness those who seek to learn about Judaism.

Classical Attitudes toward Conversion and Converts
Some people think that conversion to Judaism is a recent phenomenon. The fact is that Jews actively sought converts in pre-Christian times and for the first several centuries of the common era, and there were many converts to Judaism. When Christianity became the official religion

of the Roman Empire, conversion to Judaism and the seeking of converts were forbidden upon penalty of death.

The medieval Jewish view toward converts varied. A positive view was expressed in the letter to Ovadia the proselyte, written by Moses Maimonides, a great twelfth-century thinker. This letter was a response to a question posed by a convert, asking if it was permissible for him to recite those prayers that begin "Our God and God of our fathers" since his ancestors were not Jews. Maimonides answered that it was perfectly appropriate because every proselyte is considered a spiritual descendant of Abraham, the first Jew.

Because Jews have faced severe persecution in various times and places, we feel a moral obligation to apprise prospective converts of the potential difficulties in being Jewish. The need to make an individual considering conversion aware of this reality is expressed in the Talmud: "A Gentile who seeks conversion nowadays is asked: 'Why do you seek it? Do you not know that Jews are now sorrowful and oppressed, banished and in exile, and plagued with sufferings?' If the answer is: 'I know . . . ,' that person is admitted."

Many people who seek conversion expect to be warmly received. Often they are—but not always. Jewish tradition teaches that prospective converts are to be turned away three times in order that they may have ample opportunity to examine deeply their reasons for conversion. While different rabbis may take various approaches, the underlying principle they all follow is the talmudic teaching that, if an individual comes seeking conversion, that person is to be pushed away with one hand while being drawn near with the other.

One of the issues with which prospective converts must deal is the relationship to their former religion. Being Jewish means adopting, not only Jewish ceremonial practices and ethical values, but also Jewish religious beliefs. For example, Judaism teaches that the Messiah has not yet come. A belief that the Messiah has come, therefore, is incompatible with the Jewish faith.

While becoming Jewish is commonly thought of as a religious conversion, it is really something more than that. Choosing Judaism is also a matter of choosing to become part of a people. This aspect of the conversion process, taking on an ethnic identity, becoming part of a history, feeling oneself part of the Jewish destiny, is, for many people, the most challenging. Some people who are converting feel that becoming part of the people of Israel is an unrealistic expectation. Some people who are born Jewish believe that it is impossible for those not born Jewish ever to become "really" Jewish although they go through a conversion ceremony. It is important to realize that becoming Jewish is a process that takes time and, in fact, is not completed at the moment of conversion. Developing feelings and building connections does not happen overnight, but in time it *can* and *does* happen.

Judaism has not been a proselytizing religion since early Christian times. We do not have a mandate to seek converts. While we believe that we have a particular relationship with God, we also assert that God's love extends to all people. As the Talmud teaches: "The righteous of all peoples have a share in the world-to-come." On the other hand, people do come seeking conversion, and we do welcome them. As a matter of fact, since the late 1970s the Reform movement has sponsored an Outreach program, one goal of which is to ease the transition into Jewish life for those choosing to become Jews.

Building a Jewish Identity

In recent years, a rising number of people, not born Jews, have chosen to join the Jewish people through conversion. Many congregations have established programs to assist these new Jews to become integrated into the Jewish community. These programs are especially helpful for single Jews-by-Choice, who don't have an extended family to function as a natural Jewish support network.

For many Jews-by-Choice, their relationship with a Jew was the original impetus to explore Judaism. The decision to raise a Jewish family was their catalyst to explore Judaism for themselves. Some people think that most people convert to Judaism just to get married. While an impending marriage with its accompanying thoughts of home building and child rearing may be the reason that some people begin to explore Judaism, it is important to realize that conversion is not a favor that one person does for another, regardless of the depth of love between them. Ultimately the choice of Judaism must be one that individuals make because it is right for them and because they believe that Judaism will be life-enhancing for them personally.

Study is an important component of the conversion process. (Indeed, conversion is a process, called *gerut,* and the person who goes through the process is referred to as a *ger* [masculine] or *gioret* [feminine].) It is often done in the context of an Introduction to Judaism class, offered in many larger communities. Alternatively, one can study on a one-to-one basis with a rabbi. The course of study generally covers such topics as holidays, customs, life-cycle events, values, prayers and ritual, Bible and Jewish texts, history, and Hebrew. In addition to completing their course of study, those who choose to convert meet individually with a rabbi. Those sessions afford the opportunity for the prospective convert and the rabbi together to explore issues raised in the class as well as personal issues. These issues may include the difficulties inherent in making the transition from one religious worldview to another and the challenge of becoming part of a religious group with both an ethnic and a faith component. These meetings may also deal with family issues that may arise.

For many of those who convert the prospect of relating to their non-Jewish family and to their former holidays is often difficult. Going home and presenting oneself as a Jew to one's family can be intimidating. Learning how to be with one's family for their holidays as an observer rather than as an active participant requires thought and internal preparation.

Becoming Jewish is more than taking an Introduction to Judaism class. There is no way that anyone can say how long a conversion process "should" take. It varies with each individual. Conversion is not merely cognitive; it is also a matter of internal change. One begins to see oneself as a Jew and to participate in the life of the community. This participation has both individual and communal aspects, such as beginning to light *Shabbat* candles, celebrating Jewish holidays, attending services, contributing to Jewish philanthropic causes, and so on. The prospective convert comes to see the world through Jewish eyes, to think like a Jew and feel like a Jew.

Conversion Rituals

How does a person actually become Jewish? Circumcision (*milah*) and ritual immersion (*tevilah*) are required in the Orthodox, Conservative, and Reconstructionist movements and are optional within the Reform movement. The Jewish tradition regards those who convert to Judaism in adulthood as Jewish newborns. (This is not to be seen as a denigration of people's former non-Jewish lives but as a recognition that their Jewish lives are just beginning.) Just as all male infants are entered into the covenant of Abraham through circumcision, so adult males who convert enter that same covenant through circumcision. Circumcision is customarily performed by a specially trained person called a *mohel*. In the case of an adult who is to be circumcised, the procedure is usually done in a hospital or physician's office, under the supervision of a *mohel* with the participation of a urologist. If a man was already circumcised as an infant, Jewish law (*halachah*) calls for *hatafat dam berit*, the taking of a single drop of blood from the penis as a sign of the covenant.

Jewish law specifies that both men and women becoming Jewish are to undergo *tevilah* (ritual immersion). This takes place in a specially constructed ritual bath (*mikveh*) or a natural body of water. Water is a symbol of birth; the individual is seen as emerging from the water as a Jewish newborn.

All of the movements insist upon *Kabbalat Ol Mitzvot*, the acceptance of the yoke of the commandments. This means that a prospective convert must become conversant enough with Jewish practice to determine that he or she will lead a Jewish life.

A formal ceremony marks the official beginning of one's Jewish life. During the course of the ceremony, the Jew-by-Choice receives his or her Hebrew name, which will be used for Jewish ceremonial occasions. One who chooses Judaism also pledges to fulfill the commandments of Judaism, often making this pledge in the form of a personal statement. A formal interview takes place in the presence of two witnesses besides the officiating rabbi. In some communities, the witnesses are also rabbis, thus constituting a *Bet Din* (rabbinical court). In other communities, synagogue leaders serve as the witnesses. Sometimes Jewish friends act as witnesses. The witnesses take an active part in the procedure by asking questions of the Jew-by-Choice.

These questions are not to be perceived as a test that has to be passed. Rather, the very presence of these witnesses and the interaction between them and the Jew-by-Choice signify the community's acceptance of the conversion.

The conversion ceremony can be private (with only the convert's nearest relatives and friends present) or public (at a *Shabbat* service, for instance). Some converts who choose a private ceremony follow it up with a public marking of their becoming Jewish (such as lighting candles or chanting Torah blessings at a *Shabbat* service).

People can choose to convert to Judaism under Orthodox, Conservative, Reform, or Reconstructionist auspices. Rabbis of the non-Orthodox movements generally recognize the validity of one another's conversions although they may differ somewhat in their approaches. Orthodox

Judaism does not recognize the authenticity of the non-Orthodox inter-pretations of Judaism. Therefore, the validity of conversion performed under non-Orthodox auspices is denied by the Orthodox community in both Israel and the Diaspora. The religious status of a child born to a woman converted under non-Orthodox auspices is also called into question by the Orthodox. Most people choose to convert under the auspices of the movement with which they are most comfortable.

In the open society in which we live, more and more people are exploring Judaism, many with the goal of ultimately converting. The household of Israel is greatly enriched by the addition of these new members of the community. In becoming Jewish, they are following in the footsteps of the biblical Ruth whose words echo down through the ages: "Your people shall be my people and your God my God."

CREATING A HOME

·14·

Bonds of Holiness: Marriage

In Judaism, marriage is seen as the ideal state. In fact, the Hebrew word for marriage is *kiddushin,* which means "holiness." The ancient rabbis taught: "Man finds his fulfillment in woman, woman finds her fulfillment in man, and both of them draw their sustenance from God." Marriage is ideal for both the man and the woman—and for the community and society.

Judaism places enormous emphasis on the importance of marriage. The Book of Genesis teaches: ". . . it is not good for a person to be alone." Asceticism is *not* an ideal of Judaism. Normative Judaism never developed a monastic lifestyle, nor are our religious leaders expected to be celibate.

Sex in the Jewish Tradition

According to Judaism, sex in itself is not sinful. Our tradition tells us that marriage is a sanctified relationship. Sex in marriage is a *mitzvah;* it is part of human fulfillment and the fulfillment of marriage, not just something necessary for procreation. Sexual relations between husband and wife are seen as a holy union. Our tradition tells us that it is a *mitzvah* to make love, especially on *Shabbat.*

This rather positive view of sexuality is not something that stems from the recent past. The following selection from the thirteenth century gives an indication of the amazing sensitivity and advanced thinking in this area:

> . . . Engage her first in conversation that puts her heart and mind at ease and gladdens her. . . . . Speak words that arouse her to passion, union, love, desire, and eros—and words that elicit attitudes of reverence for God, piety, and modesty. Tell her of pious and good women who gave birth to fine and pure children. . . . Speak with her words, some of love, some of erotic passion, some of piety and reverence. . . . Hurry not to arouse passion until her mood is ready; begin in love; let her orgasm take place first. . . .

Sensitivity toward the sexual needs of the wife was but one aspect of a more general awareness of what makes a good marriage. We read the following statements in classical Jewish texts:

> Woman was not created from man's head, that she should dominate him, or from his feet, that he should dominate her, but from his side, that they should be equal partners.

> Your wife has been given to you in order that you may realize with her life's great plan; she is not yours to vex or grieve. Vex her not for God notes her tears.

> A wife is the joy of man's heart.

> A man should eat less than he can afford and should honor his wife and children more than he can afford.

> A man should be careful not to irritate his wife and cause her to weep.

> If your wife is short, bend down and whisper to her.

> He who loves his wife as himself, who honors her more than himself, who rears his children in the right path, and who marries them off at the proper time of their life, concerning him it is written: And you will know that your home is peace.

> Man should ever be mindful of the honor of his wife for she is responsible for all the blessings found in his household.

A man must not cause his wife to weep for God counts her tears.

Strive to fulfill your wife's wishes for it is equivalent to doing God's will.

These statements were written by men to be read by other men. This fact makes these statements all the more remarkable for their sensitivity to women's needs.

The Wedding Ceremony

The beginning of a Jewish marriage is the wedding ceremony. The central symbol of the Jewish wedding ceremony is the *chupah* (marriage canopy). It can be a *talit* held up by four poles or a specially designed canopy made of such fabric as silk, velvet, or linen. Some couples choose a floral canopy for their *chupah*. What is the symbolism of the *chupah*? The *chupah* stands for the bridal chamber and, by extension, the home that the couple is establishing.

In talmudic times, marriages took place in one of three ways: by a written document, by the man giving the woman something of value, or by physical consummation of the relationship. Any one of these modes was efficacious if done in the presence of two witnesses. (In the case of the third mode, eyewitness testimony was not allowed; witnessing by inference was accepted.)

Today, elements of all three modes have found their way into the wedding ceremony. The third mode is symbolically suggested by the presence of the *chupah*. The written document is the *ketubah,* and the item of value is the ring.

The *ketubah* is a marriage contract, traditionally written in Aramaic, signed by two witnesses. Originally, it served as a protection of the wife's interests. In it, the husband promises to provide for his wife's physical and emotional needs. The *ketubah* itself is a beautifully illuminated manuscript. In fact, among the most treasured items in the collections of Jewish museums are *ketubot* from various countries and ages. Modern *ketubot* range from inexpensive printed certificates to beautifully executed and individually created art pieces. The texts on them range from the traditional Aramaic to modern formulas expressive of a more egalitarian relationship. Some couples, with the guidance of their rabbi, choose to compose their own text.

Ketubah; Trino, Italy, 1798. From the collection of the Hebrew Union College Skirball Museum, photography by Marvin Rand.

Traditionally, the groom (*chatan*) presents a ring to the bride (*kalah*). Today, most couples exchange rings. By custom, the wedding band is unjeweled—a practice that came about originally to avoid the possibility of acquiring a wife by fraudulent means. Since discernment of the true value of a jewel requires expert knowledge, it was decided to avoid potential pitfalls by using an unjeweled ring. Reform, and some Conservative, rabbis will permit the use of a jeweled band. Although practices vary, the ring is generally placed on the right index finger. (After the ceremony, it is transferred to the ring finger of the left hand.)

Jewish wedding ceremonies can take place in a variety of settings. People may get married at home; in a synagogue; at a hotel, a hall, or a restaurant; or outdoors.

Immediately prior to the wedding ceremony, the *ketubah* is signed by the two witnesses and, often, by the rabbi, bride, and groom as well. Some couples choose to have a formal veiling ceremony (known as *badeken*) at this point. The groom places the veil over the bride's face, and a blessing is recited. The custom of *badeken* stems from the biblical story of Jacob who was tricked into marrying Leah, the older sister of Rachel, the woman he loved. Therefore, the Jewish tradition is that the groom sees the bride immediately prior to the wedding ceremony. In this way, the groom is ensured that he is marrying the bride of his choice.

The wedding begins with a procession. Generally, the attendants march in first and stand near the *chupah*. The bride and groom are each accompanied to the *chupah* by their parents, who stand under the *chupah* with them during the ceremony. There is no "giving away" of the bride, nor does the bride promise to obey her husband. The bride stands to the groom's right under the *chupah*. This is based on the biblical statement that the queen is at the king's right hand, and on their wedding day bride and groom are like queen and king.

The ceremony begins with an opening prayer and traditional phrases of greeting to bride and groom. In some ceremonies, the bride and groom share a cup of wine at this point. This cup of wine is a reminder of *erusin*, the ancient formal ceremony of engagement. In those days, this ceremony formally bound the couple. After a year had elapsed, their marriage was sealed with the ceremony of *nisuin*. In the course of time, *erusin* and *nisuin* developed into our modern wedding ceremony called *kiddushin*. The rabbi usually chooses this moment to say a few words to the couple. According to Jewish law, the bride and groom must enter the marriage willingly and without reservation. Therefore, the rabbi asks them to express their commitment to each other. Next, the groom places the ring on the bride's finger and recites: *"Harei at mekudeshet li, betaba'at zo kedat Mosheh veyisrael"* (With this ring, be consecrated unto me according to the law of Moses and Israel). In double-ring ceremonies, the bride places the ring on the groom's finger and makes a similar vow.

The *ketubah* is often read aloud by the rabbi. Attention is then focused on the cup of wine that the couple will share. Often couples will choose a cup before the wedding that will be used, not only at the ceremony, but in their home on Sabbaths and festivals. By drinking the wine together, the husband and wife are symbolically indicating that they will share all of life together. Prior to drinking the wine, the *Sheva*

Berachot (seven blessings) are chanted or recited. Among the many themes included in these seven blessings are an expression of the utter and pure joy felt by the universe at the uniting of the bride and groom and the idea that the union and flourishing of this couple are seen as a paradigm for the union and flourishing of the entire Jewish people.

The couple is pronounced married and is blessed by the rabbi. The groom steps on a glass, and everyone yells *"Mazal tov"* (good luck/ congratulations). What is the reason for breaking the glass? Nobody knows for sure. Therefore, lots of explanations have arisen. The most frequently cited is that we break the glass as a reminder of the destruction of the ancient Temple in Jerusalem. Even at times that are very personal, we do not lose sight of the fact that we are connected to our people and its history. Another interpretation is that, on the wedding day, bride and groom may be inclined to be self-centered. The breaking of the glass underfoot is a reminder that the world about us is crumbling and that we must never forget our responsibility to help repair this broken world.

Immediately after the breaking of the glass, the bride and groom kiss. After they have left the *chupah*, they go into a private room to share a few moments alone together. This is called *yichud*.

Marriage Customs

Several other customs may surround the wedding. The *aufruf* is the *aliyah* given to the bridegroom or to the couple on the *Shabbat* preceding the wedding. A special blessing (*Mi Sheberach*) is made for the couple, after which they may be showered with candy thrown by the congregation. In some congregations, instead of being called up for an *aliyah,* the bride and groom are called to the *bimah* for a prenuptial blessing.

There is a tradition for brides to go to the *mikveh* prior to the wedding. Some couples fast on the day of the wedding (before the ceremony). These customs relate to the viewing of one's wedding day as the beginning of a new period in one's life, which should be entered in a state of purity.

It is customary for the bride to wear a veil at the wedding ceremony while some grooms wear a *talit* (prayer shawl). This *talit* is sometimes a gift from the bride. Traditionally, the groom wears a *kittel* (a white robe). Another custom is for the bride to walk around the groom seven times under the *chupah* before the ceremony begins. We have mentioned several of these wedding customs because some or all of them may be observed at Jewish weddings although they are by no means universally practiced throughout the Jewish community.

While customs regarding the wedding may vary, one thing is certain: A wedding is an occasion to be celebrated fully and joyously. Rejoicing with the bride and groom is a *mitzvah*. Usually the celebration takes the form of a festive meal, which often includes Jewish, Israeli, and contemporary music and dancing. It is not uncommon for bride and groom (and their parents, too) to be lifted on chairs and held aloft while family and friends dance around them. Since the celebration is a *seudah shel mitzvah* (a meal marking the observance of a precept), it generally begins with a *Motzi* over a beautifully braided, large *chalah*.

In other words, a wedding is a real *simchah!* A *simchah* is a happy event—an occasion of joy that fills the heart and that one wishes to share with family and friends.

Divorce

Unfortunately, not every marriage is a success. While marriage is the ideal, Judaism recognizes that marriages can fail. Divorce is recognized as a last resort—but an acceptable resort. The Torah explicitly allows for divorce. Jewish divorce customs have changed over time, primarily to protect the woman. As a matter of fact, the *ketubah* actually contains the divorce settlement so that a man would think twice before divorcing his wife. A principle going back to the eleventh century is that a wife can be divorced only with her consent.

While the Orthodox and Conservative movements require a *get* (a bill of divorcement written according to Jewish law) before an individual can be remarried, the Reform movement generally does not. Sometimes Reform Jews will obtain a *get* so that they may be able to be married by an Orthodox or Conservative rabbi in the future and so that the status of their future children is not in jeopardy. Many Reform Jews are disturbed by one particular aspect of Jewish divorce law: namely, it is the man who gives the divorce; it is not an equal procedure.

Even as we discuss divorce, it is in terms of a remarriage because, after all, in Judaism marriage does remain the ideal. Marriage can bring us true fulfillment and an abundance of blessings: joy and happiness, love and companionship, peace and friendship.

[Acknowledgment: Roland B. Gittelsohn, *Love, Sex, and Marriage: A Jewish View.* (New York: Union of American Hebrew Congregations, 1980)]

·15·

Establishing a Jewish Home

When we think of marriage, we think of love, a wedding, and "living happily ever after." We sometimes don't think of the fact that, in getting married, we are also making a commitment to establish a Jewish home together.

What does this term "Jewish home" really mean? Is a Jewish home merely a home in which a Jew lives? Certainly, that's a beginning, but there is more to it. A Jewish home contains a variety of Jewish objects and is pervaded by a Jewish spirit.

The Mezuzah

One way to show a commitment to Judaism is by placing a *mezuzah* on the doorpost of the home. Some Jews place the *mezuzah* only at the front door while others place a *mezuzah* on the right doorpost of each room in the house (except the bathrooms).

A *mezuzah* is a holder, usually wood, ceramic, or metal, that contains a handwritten scroll (*klaf*) on which are inscribed passages from Deuteronomy 6:4–9 and 11:13–21. Why these particular passages? These passages contain such central precepts of Judaism as the unity of God, the love of God, and the importance of learning the Jewish tradition and transmitting it to one's children. In those same biblical passages, we are enjoined to write down those precepts and place them on the door-

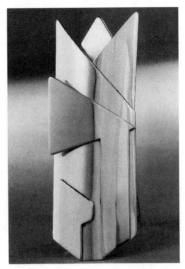

Mezuzah, Moshe Zabari; 20th century. From the collection of the Hebrew Union College Skirball Museum, photography by Marvin Rand.

posts of our home. The *mezuzah* has no magical power. Rather it serves as a reminder to all who enter and leave the house that they are to aspire to holiness. (Some Jews follow the custom of touching the *mezuzah* and kissing the fingers that touched the *mezuzah* whenever they enter or leave the house.)

A blessing is said when the *mezuzah* is hung. It is also customary to bring bread and salt to a house when people move in. Some people combine the *mitzvah* of hanging the *mezuzah* and the custom of bringing the bread and salt as part of a *Chanukat Habayit* (dedication of the house) ceremony.

If asked, most Jews would say that the *mezuzah* is the symbol of a Jewish home. There are, however, many other objects that contribute to the Jewish atmosphere of a home.

Ritual Objects

The fact that most Jewish holidays have ritual objects associated with them gives us ample opportunity to add an aesthetic dimension to our celebration of the holidays. On *Shabbat* and festivals we use candlesticks and a *Kiddush* cup. The *chalah* can be placed on a special tray or board and covered with a beautifully embroidered or woven cloth. The *Havdalah* ceremony at the end of the Sabbath and festivals calls for a spice box and a braided candle. In many homes, before lighting Sabbath or holiday candles, *tsedakah* is put into a *pushke* (a container for collecting money to be used for charitable purposes). On Passover, ceremonial foods are placed on a *seder* plate and the *matzah* is covered with a special cloth. A *Chanukiah* (*Chanukah menorah*) holds the candles for *Chanukah*. In addition, some people might have a special plate for apples and honey at *Rosh Hashanah, etrog* containers for *Sukot,* special flags for *Simchat Torah,* and *groggers* for *Purim.*

Judaism teaches that, when we perform a *mitzvah,* we should do it in the most beautiful way possible. For this reason, these ceremonial objects are often seen not merely as practical but as *objets d'art.* This doesn't mean that they must be very expensive. Beautiful Judaica can be found at almost any price. Sometimes people make their own ritual objects, and these can be the most meaningful of all. In Jewish preschools and religious schools, children create Judaica for their homes. How lovely it is to celebrate *Chanukah* with a *menorah* made by a three-year-old or to sit at a *Shabbat* table graced by a *chalah* cover decorated by a seven-year-old!

A Jewish atmosphere in a home comes not only from ritual objects; a Jewish home typically is filled with such books as a Bible and a prayer book as well as books about Jewish history, philosophy, and culture. Jewish magazines and newspapers are means of keeping informed of events affecting the Jewish community. Jewish art and music add an aesthetic dimension to the home.

While these items enhance a Jewish home, they do not define it. It is the spirit that pervades the home—a spirit reflecting Jewish values—that makes it a Jewish home. The spirit can best be summed up in three words: commitment, connectedness, and concern.

Those who live in a truly Jewish home have made a commitment to celebrating Judaism in their home and to having it present in their daily life. In addition to the Sabbath and festival observances we have discussed, some Jews choose to express their Jewish commitment by observing *kashrut,* the Jewish dietary laws.

Kashrut: The Jewish Dietary Laws

What are the elements of *kashrut?* (These are broad outlines only; the dietary laws are quite detailed.) Only the meat from certain animals or certain parts (the forequarters of permitted four-legged animals) of animals is allowed to be eaten. Four-legged animals that have cloven hoofs and chew their cud, fish with scales and fins, and fowl are permitted. Birds of prey are prohibited. Foods that are not kosher (fit for eating) are commonly referred to as *treif.*

The Torah understands the essense of life to be in the blood and, therefore, mandates that blood not be eaten. Specific methods of slaughtering animals and preparing meat were developed to remove the blood to the greatest extent possible. The *shochet* (ritual slaughterer) must slaughter the animal in the most humane way possible. Finally the meat is soaked and salted to remove any vestiges of blood. Kosher meat is bought from a kosher butcher.

In a kosher home, separate sets of dishes and utensils are used for dairy (*milchig*) and meat (*fleishig*) foods. There are "meat" meals and "dairy" meals. Foods containing dairy products and foods containing meat products are not eaten at the same meal. Vegetables, fruits, and foods that contain neither dairy nor meat products are *pareve* and may be used with either meat or dairy.

Why do people observe *kashrut?* There are many reasons. Some would say *kashrut* should be observed because it is God's commandment. Others might say that *kashrut* serves as a powerful reinforcement of Jewish identity. Still others might cite the ethical implications of *kashrut* (e.g., reverence for all life). Others might cite the *mitzvah* of hospitality and say that by maintaining a kosher kitchen they are enabling family and friends—indeed all Jews—including those who observe *kashrut* to eat in their home.

Orthodox and Conservative Judaism expect their adherents to observe *kashrut* while for Reform Jews it is an option. While not feeling committed to observing all the fine details of *kashrut,* some Jews feel that their Jewish life is enhanced by following some of the dietary laws.

The Home as a Repository of Jewish Values

Living Jewishly implies not living in isolation. A Jew is connected to all of the generations that came before and those that are to follow. A Jew forges a link in this chain of Jewish history by making connection with the Jewish community. This is done by becoming active in the synagogue and other Jewish institutions, both religious and communal. Jewish life has been perpetuated by commitment to the value of community. This sense of connectedness is clearly expressed by the teaching of the ancient sage Hillel: "Do not separate yourself from the community."

A sense of concern permeates a Jewish home and radiates outward. Each person in a Jewish home strives to be a *mentsh,* a caring, concerned human being. That concern extends to the other members of the family as they strive to create a loving, supportive relationship with each other. In fact, *shelom bayit* (peace in the house) is an important Jewish value. But Jews have a responsibility that extends far beyond the walls of their own houses. Jews are part of a worldwide family and, as such, feel a duty to support one another. Judaism also has a universalist message: Jews are part of the human family. All people are brothers and sisters and, therefore, have a responsibility to each other. Judaism speaks of this responsibility as *tikkun olam,* repairing the brokenness in our world. Living in a Jewish home, therefore, contributes to our individual well-being and contributes to the well-being of the world.

·16·

A Lifetime of Learning

You shall love the Lord your God with all your mind, with all your strength, with all your being. Set these words, which I command you this day, upon your heart. Teach them faithfully to your children; speak of them in your home and on your way, when you lie down and when you rise up. Bind them as a sign upon your hand; let them be a symbol before your eyes. Inscribe them on the doorposts of your house, and on your gates. Be mindful of all My *mitzvot,* and do them: so shall you consecrate yourselves to your God.

(*Gates of Prayer,* pp. 251–252)

This passage, taken from Deuteronomy 6:5–9, along with a passage from Numbers 15:40–41, is a core element in Jewish evening and morning worship. In Judaism, there is virtually no dividing line between "religion" and "study." The prayer book contains many passages from the Bible and rabbinic literature. Jews are expected to set aside time each week to study the weekly Torah portion. As the ancient sage Hillel taught: "Do not say 'When I have leisure, I will study.' Perhaps you will never have any leisure."

The Importance of Learning in the Jewish Tradition

The Deuteronomy passage, called the *Ve'ahavta* from its first Hebrew word, meaning "You shall love," teaches us that love of God and learning are closely related. True religion must have a basis in knowledge. While passing on our heritage to the next generation is an obligation, we are commanded first to learn Torah ourselves; only then will we be able to teach our children. Furthermore, learning can and should take place anywhere and everywhere. By no means must it be confined to a formal classroom setting.

A well-known rabbinic dictum tells us that "an ignorant person cannot be pious." A person who is not Jewishly knowledgeable cannot fully participate in Jewish life. Knowledge does not come by osmosis. Learning is one thing that cannot be bequeathed. It must be acquired by each individual.

What is the process of acquiring Jewish education? Before they receive any *formal* Jewish education, children begin to build their Jewish identities by what they experience at home. Colorful celebrations of *Shabbat* and holidays leave vivid impressions on young minds and hearts. Hearing Jewish music and learning to sing simple Hebrew songs make Judaism enjoyable and an integral aspect of a child's life. Having Jewish art and symbols in their homes creates an organic Jewish atmosphere in their young lives. The Hebrew words for "Torah," "parent," and "teacher" all come from the same root. Certainly, for the very young, the most effective teacher of Torah is the parent. One's basic values and attitudes towards life are acquired in the home. While parents are our first teachers, there will be many other teachers in our lives, and Judaism accords them special honor. Learning and scholarship are supremely valued in the Jewish tradition.

Most children receive their formal Jewish education in a synagogue religious school, attending after-school (sometimes called Hebrew school or *cheder*) and/or weekend classes (sometimes referred to as Sunday school). In these classes, they study Hebrew, Bible, and Jewish history. They celebrate Jewish holidays, discuss contemporary issues as they relate to Jews, and reinforce Jewish values. The students experience Jewish culture via art, music, dance, drama, and literature.

Several kinds of synagogue professionals assist in the education of children and adults. In addition to being the spiritual leader of the congregation, the rabbi has overall responsibility for the temple's educational program. In fact, the word "rabbi" means "teacher" and much of the rabbi's role is teaching, in formal and informal settings. The day-to-day operation of the synagogue's religious school and other educational programing, in many congregations, is the job of the temple educator. The musical portion of religious services is led by the cantor, who often also directs the music program of the school.

Every religion has ceremonies to mark rites of passage. Ceremonies mark important learning milestones: Consecration marks the beginning of formal Jewish study, *Bar/Bat Mitzvah* the entry into adolescence, and Confirmation the approach of adulthood.

Consecration

Consecration generally takes place at the beginning of kindergarten; some congregations, however, will consecrate all new students entering the primary department or, alternatively, those beginning Hebrew language study. The ceremony is often held as part of the *Simchat Torah* celebration. In some temples, a large *talit* (prayer shawl) is held over the students while they sing a song and recite the *Shema* (the basic declaration of Jewish faith: Hear, O Israel: the Lord is our God, the Lord is One—Deuteronomy 6:4). The children are blessed by the rabbi and are given a certificate and a miniature Torah.

Bar/Bat Mitzvah

The word *mitzvah* means "commandment." From the age of thirteen, Jews are obligated to observe the commandments, to perform the *mitzvot* of the Torah. That is the meaning of *Bar Mitzvah*. It is a status a boy achieves automatically—he becomes *Bar Mitzvah* (one obligated to perform *mitzvot*). *Bar Mitzvah* is a noun, not a verb. It is incorrect to say: "I was *Bar Mitzvah*ed." This error is often made.

While the *status* of the *Bar Mitzvah* is attained automatically, the *ceremony* marking that attainment requires preparation, including several years of Hebrew and Judaic studies. If that preparation process is not completed prior to the thirteenth birthday, the ceremony will be postponed. It can take place anytime after thirteen, even well into adulthood. As a matter of fact, in recent years it has become quite common for adults to have a *Bar Mitzvah* celebration as the culmination of an adult study program.

The *Bar Mitzvah* ceremony itself dates back to the Middle Ages; it is not biblical or talmudic in origin as some people think. Though the details of the ceremony will vary from congregation to congregation, there are some common elements. The *Bar Mitzvah* (as the young man is called) will usually conduct some portion of the service. He will read or chant a portion from the Torah (the first five books of the Bible), a *haftarah* (concluding reading, from the Prophets section of the Bible), and the blessings before and after these readings. He will make a speech or offer a personal prayer. In many communities, this is the first time he will wear a *talit*. The rabbi will speak to him about the significance of the occasion and will bless him. He will receive a certificate and a gift of some ritual object or book from the synagogue.

Most parents host a party in honor of the *Bar Mitzvah*. While the reception is a lovely family event, it is secondary to the essential element in the celebration, the service. To commemorate this milestone, an act of *tsedakah*—such as a gift to the temple—is appropriate.

The ceremony that marks the coming of age for girls is called *Bat* (or *Bas*) *Mitzvah*. Though technically a girl achieves her religious majority at twelve (a recognition that girls mature faster), most temples observe the *Bat Mitzvah* at thirteen. The *Bat Mitzvah* ceremony basically corresponds to the *Bar Mitzvah*, though congregational customs vary. The custom of having a *Bat Mitzvah* ceremony for girls is about sixty years old and has gained popularity within the last two decades. It is now almost universally practiced in Reform, Conservative, and Reconstructionist synagogues; some Conservative congregations, however, do not allow girls to read from the Torah. Generally, Orthodox synagogues do not have a *Bat Mitzvah* ceremony; those that do conduct it very differently from the ceremonies of Reform, Conservative, and Reconstructionist synagogues.

At *Bar/Bat Mitzvah*, students make a commitment to continue their Jewish education. Study is a lifelong *mitzvah*. *Bar/Bat Mitzvah* is in no way to be considered a graduation from Jewish studies.

Confirmation

Confirmation is a group ceremony, which generally takes place on *Shavuot* in Reform, many Conservative, and some modern Orthodox synagogues. The Confirmation class has studied together for several years. The final year (usually, the tenth grade) is often taught by the rabbi and/or temple educator. The Confirmation ceremony marks the completion of a prescribed course of study in a temple school. The confirmands are confirming their intention to live their lives as Jews. The ceremony may include the reading from the Torah (the Ten Commandments), a cantata or drama, special music, speeches, a floral offering, and a blessing of the confirmands by the rabbi. In some communities, advanced Hebrew programs take students through the high school years.

While the majority of American Jewish children get their formal religious training in synagogue schools, many thousands attend Jewish day schools. These may be affiliated with a religious movement, or they may be community sponsored. In day schools, pupils concentrate on both Judaic studies and secular academics each day.

Informal Jewish Education

Children's Jewish knowledge and identity can be reinforced in informal educational settings, as well as by religious schooling. Many temples and Jewish community centers sponsor summer day camps; movement-sponsored resident camps provide a Jewish living atmosphere. Youth groups are also an important means of informal education. They fulfill social, cultural, and educational functions.

Much has been written about Jewish education for children. However, suppose you didn't receive any Jewish education as a child or suppose your Jewish education was inadequate. Does that mean that you are forever to be left outside the full orbit of Jewish life? No! There are Jewish educational opportunities, formal and informal, for adults. Many synagogues conduct adult education classes and often provide opportunities for whole families to learn together. Among the latter are special Sabbath programs for celebration and study (*Shabbatonim*) and weekend conclaves (*kallot*). Fellowship groups (*chavurot*) also sponsor study and discussion sessions. Many colleges and universities offer courses in Judaica.

Israel provides rich opportunities for increasing one's Jewish knowledge and commitment. There are ample opportunities for learning while on a visit to Israel. Among these would be organized tours for a shorter trip and *ulpanim* (intensive Hebrew seminars) for those remaining in Israel for a more extended period.

Jewish education is more than religious school, *Bar/Bat Mitzvah,* and Confirmation. It is not just for children. It can and should be a lifelong pursuit for every Jew. Jewish education not only enriches the life of the individual; it is the major insurance for the continuity of Jewish life.

TRANSITION

·17·

The Eternal Mystery: Death

Judaism is a life-affirming religion that focuses on the here-and-now. At the same time, it helps us come to grips with our finitude. It does this by providing us with a structure within which we can focus on and deal with many complicated feelings we have about death—our own as well as the death of those we love.

People look to religion to answer such ultimate questions as: "What happens to us after we die?" Judaism does not offer one single unified belief. We do not claim to know exactly what happens to us after we die. Believing in God, we leave this domain to God. While some individual Jews may believe that "dead is dead," Judaism asserts that death is not the end.

Jewish Concepts of the Afterlife
Virtually every concept of the afterlife has at one time or another found its way into Jewish tradition. An early biblical concept is that of *Sheol,* which was understood as the netherworld, a world of shadows, where the deceased were thought to dwell. A later view was that of *Gan Eden* (literally, the Garden of Eden), paradise, and *Gehinnom* (literally, the Valley of Hinnom), a place of punishment. These indicate a concept of reward and punishment after death. The idea of *Gan Eden* suggested that the righteous would be returned to a perfect primordial

place. *Gehinnom* is named for an actual place outside the Old City of Jerusalem where, in biblical times, the pagan inhabitants of the land offered their children as sacrifices. Thus that site acquired the reputation of being the most abhorrent place imaginable. While *Gehinnom* was considered a place of punishment, the sentence was for a limited period rather than eternal perdition. The notion of reward and punishment in the afterlife, referred to as *olam haba* (the world-to-come), underlies many of the teachings in the Talmud and Midrash.

The concept of physical resurrection (the bodies of all those that have died will be brought back to life on earth again) is found in the Talmud. According to traditional belief, this resurrection is to take place when the Messiah comes.

The notion of reincarnation has existed for many centuries. Some religions have wholeheartedly embraced it while others have thoroughly rejected it. While it is not a tenet of Judaism, there is precedent within Judaism for accepting the idea since a belief in reincarnation is found in many Jewish mystical texts.

Judaism asserts that the soul is immortal. Upon the death of the body, the soul returns to its Source. This is expressed in the Bible in the words of Ecclesiastes: "The dust returns to the earth as it was, and the spirit returns to God who gave it." Many Jews today hold the view that we live on through the deeds we have done and in the memories of the people whose lives we have touched. Judaism recognizes that, for human beings, memory is a very potent force. The Book of Proverbs states: "The memory of the righteous is a blessing." On the basis of this verse, it is customary when mentioning the name of one who has died to add the phrase *zichrono livrachah* (may his memory be a blessing) or *zichronah livrachah* (may her memory be a blessing).

Having briefly sketched some of the speculations concerning the afterlife, we now turn our attention to how Jews deal with the reality of death. There are many customs and practices that we will discuss. For the sake of clarity, we will divide the material as follows: Before the funeral, what mourners do, and comforting the mourners.

Before the Funeral

The concept of *Kevod Hamet* (honor due to the dead) underlies all Jewish burial customs. We honor the dead by burying them quickly (within twenty-four hours, unless *Shabbat* or a festival intervenes, or family members coming from a great distance cannot arrive in time). According to *halachah,* the body should never be left alone before burial. It is customary that a *shomer,* a person who stays in the same room as the deceased, remains throughout the night reciting psalms.

Different cultures have developed ways in which to show respect for the dead. The Jewish way to honor the dead is by *not* putting them on display, as this may seem an invasion of their privacy. Traditionally, no embalming or cosmetology is done, and the casket remains closed.

Jews recognize that death is a great equalizer. The principle of equality is enunciated in the Talmud (*Moed Katan* 27a-b): "Formerly food was brought in silver and gold baskets to the house in which a wealthy person had died and in simple willow baskets to the house in which a poor person died. The poor felt shamed. It was decreed that, out of deference to the poor, food should be brought to *all* mourners in simple willow baskets." Following this principle, certain practices were developed that insured that people were treated equally. For instance, all were prepared for burial in the same way: a ritual washing (*taharah*) and burial shrouds (*tachrichim*), including a *talit* (prayer shawl) for men. (Very often, Reform Jews will be buried in their own clothes, perhaps including a prayer shawl).

Halachah prescribes an all-wood coffin because it allows nature to take its course, unlike other types of coffins that may retard the process. Some Reform Jews may opt for coffins that are not all wood. In Israel, no coffins are used at all; the dead are buried directly in the earth. The time-honored method of honoring the dead is burial in the earth. This derives from the biblical statement that ". . . the body returns to the earth as it was. . . ." Some Reform Jews choose entombment, but the Orthodox insist on burial in the earth. Cremation is another option within Reform. However, the Orthodox do not countenance cremation. One reason is that, according to tradition, the bones must remain intact in anticipation of resurrection.

In the past, the dead were always prepared for burial by a society of laypersons known as a *Chevrah Kadisha.* Today, that task is usually performed by Jewish mortuaries. Some families that use a Jewish mortuary will request the services of a *Chevrah Kadisha* for the ritual preparations. Jews are usually buried in specially consecrated Jewish cemeteries. Some people wish to be buried in Israel; others show attachment to Israel by having some Israeli soil buried with them.

Very often, hospitals will encourage the survivors to permit an autopsy. How does Judaism regard autopsies? The general principle is that autopsies are to be avoided. Judaism holds that the human being is created in the image of God and, therefore, to do anything—even after death—to diminish the sanctity of the body is considered wrong. In certain cases an autopsy must be performed (e.g., when it is ordered by the county medical examiner). There are some other cases when Jewish law would allow this type of postmortem examination (e.g., when it could lead directly to the saving of another person's life). Some Jews are of the opinion that, if an autopsy could eventually lead to the saving of lives, it is a valid reflection of Jewish values; other Jews strictly hold that the autopsy may be performed only if it is likely to save the life of a specific patient.

The saving of life is of paramount importance in Judaism. In recent years, the transplantation of organs has saved lives. What, then, is the Jewish view covering organ transplants?

This subject is extremely complex. Because the technology is changing so rapidly, Judaism must continue to evaluate its response to specific questions. However, we can cite an underlying principle: We should do what we can to prolong the life of an individual. Therefore, while we may not shorten the life of a donor, we may transplant organs after the death of a donor so that another individual may have a chance for a longer and more productive life. Thus we learn that Jewish tradition places tremendous value on human life and does not permit the taking of a life. Active euthanasia is prohibited. This talmudic principle applies: While we are not allowed to hasten death, neither is it necessary for us to prevent death from coming.

Similarly, Judaism opposes suicide. In fact, at one time, the bodies of those who committed suicide were buried in disgrace. Aware of the pain of the survivors, Jewish authorities have usually allowed full burial honors to a suicide by recognizing that the act was one of temporary insanity.

What Mourners Do

Judaism attempts to guide the mourner through a process that expresses the deepest respect and honor for the one who has died and aids the mourner to grieve, to accept the loss, and, finally, to return fully to life. According to Jewish law, there are seven relatives for whom one is obligated to mourn: father, mother, brother, sister, son, daughter, and spouse. Of course, one is permitted to mourn for others not in these categories.

When death occurs, a traditional practice is to cover the mirrors in the house, perhaps because the mourning period should not be a time for vanity.

Funeral services normally take place in the chapel of a mortuary or cemetery. We don't send flowers to a Jewish funeral. Instead we memorialize the dead through a contribution to some worthy cause. A rabbi usually officiates, but a rabbi's presence is not a Jewish requirement. A eulogy honoring the memory of the person and bringing comfort to the mourners is a focal point of the service. The eulogy is generally delivered by the rabbi although it may be offered by a friend or family member. The funeral service includes the reading or chanting of selected psalms and prayers, including the *El Malei Rachamim,* a prayer that asks for the repose of the soul of the departed.

At graveside, the ceremony of *Keriah* (tearing) is performed. The custom of tearing one's clothing as an expression of one's grief goes back to biblical times. In Genesis 37:34, "Jacob rent his clothes . . . and observed mourning for his son many days." It is a way of physically acting out the way we feel—torn. *Keriah* is performed by tearing the mourner's garment (e.g., a shirt or blouse). Some Jews tear a black ribbon instead of their clothing. The ripped garment or ribbon is worn throughout the week of mourning (*Shivah*). Some wear it for thirty days after the funeral.

After some brief prayers, the actual burial takes place. It is customary for family and friends to pay their last respects to the deceased by assisting in the burial. This is done by filling the grave with shovelsful of earth. The funeral ends with the mourners reciting *Kaddish,* a prayer that, interestingly, doesn't mention death but rather praises God and expresses the hope for a world at peace.

The prescribed stages of mourning reflect the various stages of grief. The first mourning period is called *Shivah* (seven) since traditionally it lasts for seven days, counting the day of the funeral as the first of the seven. Some Reform Jews observe only three days. Immediately after the funeral, the mourners return to the house where the family will be "sitting *Shivah.*" Before entering the house, they pour water over their hands from a pitcher that has been set by the door. This is also done by any friends who were at the cemetery and are coming back to the house to console the mourners. When the mourners enter the house, a *Shivah* candle, provided by the funeral home, is lit. It remains burning throughout the *Shivah* period.

You may have heard the expression "sitting *Shivah.*" This term comes from the practice of not sitting in one's comfortable chair during this time of loss but rather sitting on a low bench, a box, or even on the floor. During the *Shivah* period, the mourner remains at home and abstains from work, Torah study, sex, and bathing for pleasure. *Kaddish* is recited daily. Since the *Kaddish* calls for a congregational response, a *minyan* is necessary. Because the mourner must remain at home, friends gather there to form a *minyan.* These mourning practices give outward expression to the inner sense of loss. On *Shabbat,* public mourning is not observed. The mourners are permitted to leave their homes to attend regular synagogue services where they recite *Kaddish.*

The period of *Shivah* is actually the first part of the thirty-day mourning period known as *Sheloshim* (thirty). During the period of *Sheloshim,* which follows *Shivah,* some restrictions still apply, but the mourner begins to return to daily activity. For instance, one returns to work but does not attend parties. The daily recitation of *Kaddish* continues.

The formal mourning period lasts for thirty days, a tradition going back to the Israelites' mourning Moses for thirty days. However, for those mourning their parents, mourning extends to a year (traditional Jews observe an eleven-month mourning period). This extended mourning period for parents can be seen as an expression of the *mitzvah* "honor your father and your mother."

It is customary to have a dedication of the grave marker (an unveiling). While this may be done anytime after *Sheloshim,* it is often scheduled at the end of the year's mourning. Some people also memorialize their departed relatives by including their names on a memorial wall or plaque in the synagogue.

We mark the *yahrzeit,* the anniversary of the death of a loved one, by lighting a twenty-four-hour memorial candle, by making a charitable contribution in memory of the departed, and by reciting *Kaddish* (generally at *Shabbat* services that week). The date of the *yahrzeit* is fixed according to the Hebrew calendar. When *Kaddish* is recited at Sabbath services, the rabbi mentions the names of those whose *yahrzeit*s are being observed. On *Yom Kippur,* we hold a service, called *Yizkor,* in memory of the departed. In Orthodox and Conservative Ashkenazic congregations, *Yizkor* is also recited as part of the festival service on the last day of *Sukot, Pesach,* and *Shavuot.* Many Reform congregations

Memorial lamp, Moshe Zabari; New York, U.S.A., 1974. From the collection of the Hebrew Union College Skirball Museum, photography by Marvin Rand.

include *Yizkor* in the festival service on the last day of *Pesach*. It is customary to light a memorial candle at sunset prior to the day when *Yizkor* is said.

Comforting the Mourners

It is a *mitzvah* to comfort mourners. This is done in a number of ways. Friends prepare the first meal that the mourners eat upon returning home from the funeral. This is called *Seudat Havra'ah,* the meal of consolation. Mindful of the fact that the mourners are immersed in their grief, friends encourage them to begin their reentry into life by eating this meal. Hard-boiled eggs and other symbols of the ongoing cycle of life are generally served. We usually bring food, often something sweet, to the house of mourning.

While some friends visit the house of mourning immediately after the funeral, it is appropriate to pay a condolence call anytime during *Shivah.* Conversation about the person who has died is appropriate and may be of comfort to the mourners. It is a *mitzvah* to go to a house of mourning during *Shivah* in order to be part of a *minyan.* In those situations where there may not be enough people for a *minyan,* temple members will come to the home to constitute one. If one lives at too great a distance to visit, it is appropriate to write a letter of condolence to the mourner.

Jewish mourning practices allow an individual who has lost a dear one to have a framework within which to express the full range of emotions connected with loss. In stages, the person emerges from the depths of grief. Jewish traditions provide a healing of the soul for the mourners, the family, and the community.

Aspects of Faith

♦ ♦ ♦

GOD
PRAYER AND LITURGY
MIDRASH

·18·

God

One of our most important prayers begins "Blessed are You, our God and God of our ancestors, God of Abraham, God of Isaac, and God of Jacob." This unusual phrasing, with its emphatic parallelism, was noticed by our ancient rabbis. We might have expected the prayer to read "God of Abraham, Isaac, and Jacob" but instead the phrase "God of . . ." appears three times. Since Judaism affirms a belief in one God, there obviously is a message here: While there is only one God, each generation and, in fact, each individual understands God differently.

This ancient Jewish insight is helpful to keep in mind as we approach the complex subject of the Jewish understanding of God. The subject is so complex because there isn't just *one* Jewish understanding of God. In fact, over the long course of our history, we Jews have held a variety of opinions concerning the nature of God.

In this chapter, we will review some ways Jews have conceived of God. Those mentioned are by no means all-inclusive; rather, they reflect a variety of possibilities within Jewish thought.

A Biblical View of God

Contemporary biblical scholars agree that the Bible contains different teachings about God.

1. *Monotheism.* This concept finds its expression in the *Shema,* the main statement of Jewish belief: Hear, O Israel: the Lord is our God, the Lord is One. God is unique; God has no parents, no offspring, no spouse.

Although God is always conceived of as one, God is referred to by a variety of such names as *Adonai* (my Lord), *Elohim* (God), *El Shaddai* (Almighty God), *YHVH* (the consonants representing the Hebrew name for God).

2. *God is not physical.* In the Ten Commandments, we are told not to make any representational form of God. Frequently, the Bible will refer to God as having human attributes: the "face" of God or the "voice" of God. While this kind of language may be used, the real underlying message is that God has no physical form that exists or can be represented. In fact, God is not restricted to any natural phenomenon. The prophet Elijah, searching for God, came to understand that God was not to be found in wind, earthquake, or fire but rather in the "still, small voice" of conscience.

3. *God in nature and history.* God is seen as the Creator of the universe. This is beautifully expressed in the Book of Psalms.

> For He spoke, and it was;
> He commanded, and it endured.
> (Psalms 33:9)

God is seen as intervening directly in history. The Ten Commandments begin with the phrase "I am the Lord your God who brought you out of the land of Egypt." This is not just a rhetorical flourish. The biblical author means to say that it was God who was responsible for freeing the Israelite slaves.

4. *God has a special relationship with Israel.* According to the Torah, the people of Israel is God's chosen people.

> For you are a people consecrated to the Lord your God: of
> all the peoples on earth the Lord your God chose you to be
> His treasured people. . . .
> (Deuteronomy 7:6)

This notion of chosenness—often misunderstood—implies special responsibility, not special privilege. The prophet Amos quoted God as saying: "You alone have I singled out of all the families of the earth. That is why I will call you to account for all your iniquities."

5. *Israel has a covenant with God.* A covenant is a sacred agreement, mutually binding all the participants. The covenant was made not only with the Jews of that generation but with those of all the generations to follow.

> I make this covenant, with its sanctions, not with you alone,
> but . . . with those who are not with us here this day.
> (Deuteronomy 29:13–14)

6. *Ethical Monotheism.* The biblical view is not simply that God is One but that the one God requires ethical behavior.

> You shall be holy because I the Lord your God am holy.
> (Leviticus 19:2)

God's expectations are clearly spelled out by the prophet Micah.

> He has told you, O man, what is good,
> And what the Lord requires of you:
> Only to do justice
> And to love goodness,
> And to walk modestly with your God.
> (Micah 6:8)

7. *God is a personal God.* While the Bible conceives of God as the Creator of the universe, at the same time it maintains that God is very close to us.

> The Lord is near to all who call Him,
> to all who call Him with sincerity.
> (Psalms 145:18)

God in Postbiblical Literature

After the completion of the Bible, Judaism continued to develop. Scholars analyzed and interpreted biblical teachings and applied them to situations that arose in contemporary life. The results of the discussions of these ancient rabbis can be found in rabbinic literature, primarily the Talmud and Midrash.

The discussions about God in rabbinic literature did not come about in a systematic way nor do they represent a systematic theology. However, there are many references to God, of course, and a number of views emerge.

The rabbis took God's existence for granted. There were no debates about the reality of God; it was a given, and the belief in one God remained unshakable. A number of new names were used to describe God: *Hakadosh Baruch Hu* (the Holy One, blessed be He), *Ribono shel Olam* (Master of the universe), *Harachaman* (the Merciful One), and *Avinu Shebashamayim* (our Father in heaven).

God is seen as the Judge of the world. God's attribute of justice is maintained but is tempered by the attribute of mercy. This view recognizes that the foundation of the world must be justice, but, if it were only justice, untempered with mercy, human beings would not be able to live in society.

The rabbis knew God as the Creator of the universe yet felt that God is very near to human beings. They explained that God spoke to Moses from a lowly thorn bush rather than from some stately tree because there is no place devoid of God's presence. They believed that God is interested in the well-being of every single person.

The Medieval Period

In the Middle Ages, a number of Jewish philosophers speculated about the nature of God. Perhaps the most influential of these was Moses Maimonides (1135–1204). Maimonides, a follower of Aristotle, taught that God exists, is one, and has no body. He believed that, while people could prove God's existence, it is impossible fully to understand God. He saw God as pure intellect and as the One who created the universe out of nothing.

A far different approach was taken by Jewish mystics. They weren't satisfied with talking about God; their goal was communion with God. The most influential of these was Isaac Luria (1534–1572). He maintained that God had originally filled all space and that the universe was created by God's contracting and, thus, allowing it to come into being. Divine light flowed into the primordial space, scattering divine sparks throughout the world.

Some Modern Views of God

One of the most influential thinkers of the twentieth century was Martin Buber, whose impact was felt in both Jewish and Christian theological circles. Buber, best known for his articulation of the "I-Thou" relationship, noted that there are different levels of human interrelatedness. When we relate to someone in order to satisfy a personal need, we are relating to that person as an object, an "it." The "I-Thou" relationship, on the other hand, is characterized by mutuality. Of necessity in life, many relations must be the "I-It" type. Yet, we are enjoined to strive for the "I-Thou" in our dealings with other people.

For Buber, God is the "Eternal Thou," ever present. God cannot be defined, described, or even proven to exist; God can only be met. Indeed, whenever we enter into a genuine relationship with another, we discover God. It is through the ordinary activities of daily life that God can be encountered.

The final two theologies we will look at take positions substantially different from those of almost every thinker preceding them. The classical theologians spoke of God as an all-powerful, all-knowing, all-good Being. Milton Steinberg, a twentieth-century rabbi, understood God as a Power and a Mind. God enters into relations with the world and particularly with people. However, he believed that God is not all-powerful. This view is one answer to the age-old question: "How could an all-powerful and all-good God create a world in which evil exists?" It exempts God from responsibility for the chance events that occur in the universe.

One of the most creative thinkers in modern Jewish life was Mordecai M. Kaplan. He taught that religion today must teach people to identify as divine whatever in human nature or in the world enhances human life. He believed that God is a force *within* the natural world rather than one that supernaturally acts *upon* nature. For Kaplan, God is the sum of everything in the world that renders life significant and worthwhile. Kaplan viewed God as a Process, not as a Being. God is not the whole universe but that aspect of the universe that brings human fulfillment.

Often, when people say that they don't believe in God, what they mean is that they don't really accept one particular concept. Judaism would say that, while there is one God, there is no one way to understand God. In fact, many different views concerning God have emerged over the long course of Jewish history. While Judaism allows for a wide range of beliefs, there are limits as to what is an acceptable Jewish view. All Jewish views maintain that God is not physical and has no divine partners. Furthermore, Judaism insists upon the absolute oneness of God.

Not only is God sacred, but even references to God take on sanctity. This is expressed in the commandment: "You shall not take the name of the Lord your God in vain." For instance, while the ancient Temple stood, the Tetragrammaton (YHVH, the four-letter name for God)—being considered so holy—was pronounced only once a year—on *Yom Kippur*—and only by the High Priest, upon emerging from the Holy of Holies to bless the people. Then, as now, the word *Adonai* (my Lord) was used in prayer as a substitute for the Tetragrammaton.

Some Jews have further extended the practice of substituting for the divine Name. When talking about God, they substitute the word *Hashem* (the Name) for *Adonai*. As a way of showing their respect for God, some Jews will actually not write out that word fully, even in English, but instead will write "G-d."

Because the Tetragrammaton has not been pronounced since the destruction of the Temple more than 1,900 years ago, the proper pronunciation of that Name is not known. Some scholars believe that it may have been Yahveh. While some people assume that Jehovah is a Jewish name for God, it clearly is not and never has been. The word Jehovah is the result of the error of reading the consonants of the Tetragrammaton with the vowels of the word *Adonai*.

This chapter has only begun to touch on several of the many Jewish concepts of God.

[Acknowledgment: For further study, Rifat Sonsino and Daniel B. Syme, Finding God. (New York: Union of American Hebrew Congregations, 1986)]

·19·

Prayer and Liturgy

In Judaism, there are both public and private aspects of prayer. Jewish prayer is both set and spontaneous. The Talmud defines prayer as the service of the heart (*Ta'anit* 2a), thus suggesting that prayer should express the deepest feelings and longings of the soul. Through our long history, these longings have taken shape and been formed into a myriad of blessings (*berachot*) for nearly every occasion, both ordinary and extraordinary, and a fixed liturgy for prescribed times and seasons.

Blessings

For instance, there is a *berachah* (blessing) for every type of food and drink. There is a blessing to be recited upon seeing wonders of nature. There is a blessing when one recovers from grave illness or survives danger. Virtually every aspect of life is marked by a blessing. Perhaps one of the most often recited blessings is the *Shehecheyanu* (Blessed are You, Eternal our God, Ruler of the universe, who has kept us alive, sustained us, and brought us to this time). This blessing provides a wonderful way to mark special occasions in our lives (e.g., the birth of a child) or a new venture or even the tasting of a season's first fruits.

In addition to blessings for various occasions, there are prayers that are recited regularly. Traditionally, Jews *daven* (pray) three times a day—evening, morning, and afternoon—and there is a fixed form to these prayers, which can be recited privately or at services in a synagogue.

Minyan

Praying with a congregation is central to Judaism. In fact, public worship is more highly valued than private prayer. This is because Judaism is more than an expression of an individual's faith in God; it is a reflection of the covenantal relationship between God and the Jewish people. A service is denoted as public worship if a *minyan* is present. A *minyan* is a quorum of ten adult Jews ("adult" being defined as thirteen years of age or older). In Orthodox synagogues, only men can constitute a *minyan*. In Reform and Reconstructionist congregations, both men and women are considered part of a *minyan*. In Conservative synagogues, the practice varies.

The notion of ten individuals as constituting a congregation has ancient roots. One *midrash* ties this practice to the story of the twelve spies sent by Moses to reconnoiter the Promised Land. Two of the spies gave an optimistic report; the other ten were reluctant to move ahead with the plans to enter Canaan. This group of ten is referred to, in the Bible, as "an evil congregation." Since the term "congregation" is applied here to ten individuals, the rabbis deduced that ten people constitute a congregation.

Prayer is not simply an exercise of the mind; it involves the heart as well. As a matter of fact, Jews traditionally involve the whole body in prayer. This is based on the scriptural verse: "Bless the Eternal, O my soul and let *all* that is within me praise God." One will commonly see worshipers *shuckling* (swaying) as they pray, particularly in Orthodox and Conservative synagogues. There are also certain points in the service when worshipers will bend the knee and bow as a sign of reverence for God.

Yarmulke, Talit, and Tefilin

Some Jews show reverence for God by wearing a *yarmulke* (skullcap). It may be worn during worship, during study, or while eating (since there are blessings recited before and after the meal). Some Jews wear a *yarmulke* all the time as a sign of respect; others choose not to wear one at all. In Reform congregations covering the head during worship is optional. In Orthodox, Conservative, and Reconstructionist synagogues, men worship with heads covered. In Orthodox and many Con-

Talit, talit bag, and tefilin bag; China, 1904. From the collection of the Hebrew Union College Skirball Museum, photography by John R. Forsman.

servative congregations married women wear hats or head coverings at services.

The wearing of a *talit* (prayer shawl) during prayer has a biblical basis. (Numbers 15:37–41) The fringes on the garment are a reminder to follow God's commandments. As in the case of the *yarmulke*, customs regarding the wearing of the *talit* vary between and within the movements.

There is a biblical basis (Deuteronomy 6:8) for the practice of wearing *tefilin* during weekday morning prayers. These prayer boxes, like the *mezuzah,* contain the *Shema* and other passages and serve as a reminder of the *mitzvot* that bind the Jew to God. As with the other worship practices, customs concerning the wearing of *tefilin* vary greatly.

The community gathers together in larger numbers for worship on Sabbaths, festivals, and the High Holy Days. Most Orthodox synagogues have a brief service at sunset on Friday and a full *Shabbat* service (including Torah reading) on Saturday morning. Many Conservative synagogues hold a family-oriented service on Friday evening and a more traditional *Shabbat* service on Saturday morning. For most Reform congregations the major *Shabbat* service takes place on Friday night, and many Reform temples have a Saturday morning service as well.

The Structure of the Shabbat Evening Service

Worshipers follow the service by reading from a *siddur* (prayer book). The word *siddur* comes from the Hebrew word meaning "order," indicating that there is a prescribed order to the service. Although certain elements of style may differ from synagogue to synagogue, here is the basic structure of the Sabbath eve worship service:

1. Candlelighting: the lighting of the Sabbath candles customarily takes place at home; in many Reform congregations it takes place at the beginning of the evening service as well.

2. *Kabbalat Shabbat:* preliminary psalms, songs, and readings to welcome *Shabbat.*

3. Reader's *Kaddish:* a praise of God, which is sung and which marks the division between parts of the service.

4. *Barechu:* the call to worship.

5. Blessings before the *Shema:* on the themes of creation and revelation.

6. *Shema:* the declaration of a Jew's faith: Hear, O Israel: the Lord is our God, the Lord is One." (The *Ve'ahavta*—"You shall love . . ."— is part of the *Shema.* These passages come from Deuteronomy 6:4–9 and Numbers 15:40–41.)

7. Redemption: includes the *Mi Chamochah* (Who is like You?) from Exodus 15:11, 18, taken from the song sung by the Israelites after crossing the Sea of Reeds from slavery to freedom.

8. *Hashkivenu:* the evening prayer.

9. *Veshamru:* passage from Exodus 31:16–17 in which the Sabbath is recognized as a sign of the covenant between God and the Jewish people.

10. *Tefilah* (also called the *Amidah* or *Shemoneh Esreh*): a series of short blessings, the *Tefilah* is the core of the service. During or after the *Tefilah,* time is given for personal silent prayer or meditation.

11. *Kiddush:* the blessing over a cup of wine, proclaiming the holiness of *Shabbat. Kiddush* customarily is chanted or recited at home before the Sabbath evening meal. It has also become part of the Sabbath evening service. Depending upon congregational custom, it is chanted after the candlelighting, before the Torah service or the sermon, or at the beginning of the *Oneg Shabbat.*

12. Torah service: the Torah is read or chanted at the *Shabbat* morning service. In many Reform congregations, it is read at the *Shabbat* evening service as well.

13. *Devar Torah:* literally, "a word of Torah," which may take the form of a sermon, talk, explication, story, discussion, program, etc.

14. *Alenu:* sometimes referred to as the "Adoration," this prayer of praise to God is sung with the congregation standing before the open ark. Worshipers traditionally bend the knee and bow during this prayer.

15. Meditation before *Kaddish.*

16. Mourner's *Kaddish:* a praise of God, recited at this point in the service in memory of those that have died. The rabbi usually reads the names of those who were buried during the past week and the names of those whose anniversary of death (*yahrzeit*) is being observed. In Orthodox and Conservative synagogues, only mourners stand for this *Kaddish;* the custom in Reform synagogues is for everyone to stand.

17. Closing song.

18. Closing prayer or benediction.

The Interplay between Fixed Liturgy and Personal Intention

Seeing that the service is so highly structured, one may well ask: "Where is the spontaneity?" In fact, in Jewish prayer there is an interplay between fixed liturgy (*kevah*) and personal intention (*kavanah*). Jewish tradition teaches that there is value in having fixed prayers. A set liturgy connects Jews today with those who lived in every age and with those who live in Jewish communities throughout the world. In every Jewish service, time is allotted for personal prayer and meditation.

Use of Hebrew

The use of Hebrew in worship is another way that we are connected to our Jewish past and to Jews in all lands today. Jews with some familiarity with the Hebrew prayers can walk into a synagogue anywhere in the world and find elements of the service with which they feel at home. Since not all Jews are fluent in Hebrew, many congregations have introduced prayers in the vernacular as well as retaining some in Hebrew. The use of the vernacular at services is not new; it dates back to talmudic times. The *Kaddish* prayer, for instance, is not in Hebrew but in Aramaic, the daily language spoken by the people at the time the prayer was formulated. The amount of Hebrew in the service varies widely from synagogue to synagogue.

Jewish Values as Expressed in Prayers

Our prayers transmit values and ideals. For instance, in the *Ve'ahavta,* which is recited at every evening and morning service, we find: "You shall love the Lord your God with all your mind, with all your strength, with all your being. Set these words, which I command you this day, upon your heart. Teach them faithfully to your children; speak of them in your home and on your way, when you lie down and when you rise up." This passage stresses the love of God, the value of learning, and the importance of transmitting Judaism to the next generation.

Not only is the *siddur* a repository of wisdom, it is also—carefully read—a record of Jewish history. Certain prayers came into the liturgy as a result of events that befell Jewish communities in the past. A widespread practice, with roots in the period of the Crusades when many Jewish communities in Europe were decimated, is the recitation of a prayer in remembrance of those that were martyred: "May God remember forever our brothers and sisters of the house of Israel, who gave their lives for the sanctification of the divine Name." This prayer is part of the memorial service on festivals.

The prayer book also serves as a record of the intellectual currents that have influenced Jewish thought throughout the ages. The well-known hymn, *Yigdal,* sets forth in an encapsulated form many tenets of Jewish philosophy. It actually puts Maimonides' Thirteen Articles of Faith into a poetic form. Among the principles enumerated are: God is eternal, God has no physical form, God is unchanging, and Moses' closeness with God was unique in human history.

These are only a few examples of the richness within the pages of the *siddur*. The reading of the prayer book is both study and prayer, and in Judaism these two activities clearly overlap.

Within Judaism, there are many different types of prayers. We offer prayers of thanksgiving and prayers of petition. Some are simply praises of God while others are reflections on our aspirations and ideals. The Hebrew word for prayer is *tefilah*, based on the verb *lehitpalel*, which means "to judge *oneself*." Thus Jewish prayer is not so much a pleading before God as a process of self-reckoning. Through prayer, we regularly assess ourselves and our relationship with others and with God.

Our rabbis were aware that because we had a structured service it would be easy to fall into a routine repetition of the prayers. They warned against this: "When you pray, do not let your prayer become routine, but let it be a sincere supplication. . . ." This means that, when we read the words of the prayer book, we should infuse them each time with new life and meaning. We must learn what the prayer has meant to past generations—but more than that what it can mean to us. As each generation in the past has brought its own insights to the text, it is for us to bring our own deepest thoughts, hopes, dreams, desires, and even fears as we confront the text. Further, the words of the prayer book and the setting of the synagogue should inspire us to offer the prayers of our own hearts as each of us attempts to reach within ourselves and beyond ourselves.

Prayer is not reserved for synagogues alone. While prayer together with the community is highly valued, individual prayer is also encouraged. Many Jews recite the *Shema* upon retiring at night and acknowledge God when they awake in the morning.

A beautiful statement found in *Midrash Tehillim* teaches: "When you pray, pray in the synagogue of your city; if you are unable to pray in the synagogue, pray in your field; if you are unable to pray in your field, pray in your home; if you are unable to pray in your home, pray on your couch; and, if you are unable to pray on your couch, meditate in your heart. This is the meaning of the verse: 'Commune with your own heart upon your bed, and be still.'" Judaism emphasizes the importance of communal worship. Sometimes people feel that they have not gotten out of a worship service as much as they ought to have gotten. It is unrealistic for us to expect that every time we attend a service we will feel as if we've been touched by God. No person can live a life made up entirely of what psychologist Abraham Maslow called "peak experiences." While we can't expect to have a unique and ineffable experience every time we attend services, there is value in being together with fellow Jews and sharing in the life of the community. The worship service need not be a metaphysical experience in order to be "successful." We have to ask ourselves what should really be the outcome of the service. Our prayer book frames the answer for us: "Who rise from prayer better persons, their prayer is answered."

·20·

Midrash

Jews have a yearly round of festivals and a way to mark the key events in the cycle of life. We also have specific ways of approaching religious texts. The primary sourcebook of Judaism is the Bible. Judaism starts with the Bible—but doesn't stop with the Bible. The Bible continually infuses all of Judaism through commentaries, Talmud, and Midrash.

Here's a small example of how this works. A well-known biblical verse, which appears three times in the Bible and has influenced Jewish practice as it developed over time, is: "You shall not boil a kid in its mother's milk." (Exodus 23:19; 34:26; and Deuteronomy 14:21) In the Talmud, this was interpreted to mean that meat and dairy products were not to be eaten together. This prohibition was extended to include separate dishes and utensils for meat and dairy meals. Many talmudic passages detail this separation and form an important segment of *kashrut,* the Jewish dietary laws. Thus, a whole system of eating grew out of this one particular biblical verse.

While entire chapters, if not books, could be written about the classical biblical commentaries (such as those by Rashi, ibn Ezra, and others), the Talmud, and the Midrash, we have chosen to focus on the Midrash as a way of elucidating the Jewish approach to Scripture.

What Is Midrash?

What is *midrash?* The word *"midrash"* is based on a Hebrew root meaning "to inquire," and *midrash* is a way of inquiring into what a biblical text might mean. The word *"midrash"* is used to describe either an individual interpretation (a *midrash*) or the collection of such interpretations (the Midrash). *Midrash* can be considered as the way the ancient rabbis read between the lines of the Bible. For instance, what did Abraham's father, Terah, do for a living? You could search Genesis high and low, and you would not find any answer. Yet every child in a Jewish religious school knows the answer. Terah was an idol maker. How do we know that? The Midrash tells us so.

There is a *midrash* about Abraham's early life. There, as a way of explaining the uniqueness of Abraham's theology and his total break with the religious views and practices of the past, the following story is told.

> Terah, Abraham's father, was an idol maker. One day, he left Abraham in charge of the store. Abraham took a stick and broke all the idols except the largest one. He put the stick into the hand of the large idol. When Terah returned, he demanded to know what had happened. Abraham responded that the big idol—in a jealous rage—had destroyed the smaller ones. Terah cried out, "Why are you making fun of me? Idols have no knowledge!" Abraham challenged his father: "Let your ears hear what your mouth is saying!"
> (*Genesis Rabbah* 38:13)

The point is clear: If idols have no knowledge and cannot act, they are unworthy of being worshiped.

The Midrash as a Key to Understanding the Jewish Mind

Why do we study the Midrash? The Midrash can often give us deeper insight into the biblical text. Bible, for Jews, is not only the words that appear on the pages of the Holy Scriptures. The Midrash—and Bible commentaries as well—have become an important part of the way in which we understand the Bible. Studying the Midrash also gives us insight into the minds of the ancient rabbis and helps us understand what their concerns were.

Why have we chosen to devote a chapter in this book to *midrash?*

Midrash is unique and is a key to understanding the Jewish mind. The Midrash shows us how Jews have studied the Bible for the past 2,000 years. It is an approach to the Bible that is uniquely Jewish.

How seriously should the Midrash be taken? Is the Midrash to be understood simply as a collection of entertaining legends? A liberal Jewish response is that we take *midrashim* seriously, but not necessarily literally. We are not so much concerned with the "truth" of the story as we are with the truths about life and values and insights into the human condition that are found within the *midrashim*. In this sense, the Midrash is holy and has become part of the Jewish biblical tradition.

The rest of this chapter is going to be a long "for instance." We'll look at a number of typical *midrashim* and highlight the aspects of Judaism that they illustrate.

Selections from the Midrash and Their Theological Implications

In the biblical story of Creation, we read that God said: "Let us make man." The question that the Midrash seeks to answer is: "Who is the 'us'?" The *midrash* says that, when the time came to create man, God consulted with the ministering angels and that is why the Bible uses the word "us." But, of course, that is not the end of the *midrash*. It goes on to say that the consultants got into a big fight as to whether man should be created at all. Some said he should be created because he would be loving and righteous. Others said he shouldn't be created because he would not be honest and his life would be filled with strife. While the argument raged, God went and created man. This *midrash* underscores God's omnipotence while recognizing human frailty.

Considering human history, the question could well be asked: "Should human beings have been created at all?" Our sages debated and finally concluded that it would have been better for people not to have been created. However, since we were, we should examine our past deeds and carefully consider our future actions. Judaism is reality-oriented. We may not be the best of all possible people living in the best of all possible worlds, but that does not free us from the responsibility of improving ourselves and our world.

Another *midrash* on the theme of Creation recognizes that God's creative power far exceeds human creativity. When a human king mints coins, they are alike. However, when the Divine Sovereign created human beings there was one prototype, Adam—yet each person is different. This *midrash* teaches the uniqueness of every individual.

Do we, then, have to read the Genesis Creation story literally? Not at all. The text teaches important lessons even if not taken literally. The *midrash* gives us insight into what we can learn from the biblical statement that only one person was created initially. It teaches the value of human life: If someone saves one person's life, it is as if an entire world has been saved. It teaches the kinship of all humanity: No one can ever say, "My ancestor was greater than yours." Finally, it reminds each of us of our own worth: Every human being can rightfully say, "For my sake was the world created."

While each individual is unique and holy, no person is perfect. The flaws in each of the great biblical figures make this very clear. Rabbinic tradition says that each one of us is created with an inclination towards good and an inclination towards evil. Yet even the inclination that is called "evil" can be regarded as beneficial in some contexts. The Midrash states: "But for the Evil Desire no man would build a house, take a wife, and beget children." Nearly two thousand years before Freud, the rabbis were actually describing the libido!

Judaism exhorts us to be concerned about the environment. Basing itself on the phrase in Genesis, "And God saw everything that He had made, and found it very good," the Midrash puts these words into God's mouth: "This is a beautiful world that I have given you. Take good care of it; do not ruin it." The Midrash further relates that, before the world was created, God kept creating worlds and destroying them. Only after creating our world was God satisfied. God then said to Adam: "This is the last world I shall make. I place it in your hands: hold it in trust."

One of the hallmarks of Judaism is a passion for justice. The first crime described in the Bible is the murder of Abel by his brother, Cain. The reader is horrified by the notion that one brother could kill another. What punishment is appropriate for such a crime? The Bible allows for capital punishment, yet that punishment was not applied in this case although the crime was so repugnant. Why? The *midrash* provides the answer: Cain had never seen death. Therefore, there was no way he could know that his attack on Abel would result in the end of Abel's life. It would not be just, then, to punish Cain with death. Instead, he was condemned to eternal wandering.

This gets Cain off the hook. But what about God? Isn't God, in some way, responsible? The Midrash approaches this troubling theological question gingerly.

Rabbi Shimon bar Yochai said: "It is difficult to say this thing, and the mouth cannot utter it plainly. Think of two athletes wrestling before the king; had the king wished, he could have separated them. But he did not so desire, and one overcame the other and killed him. The victim, before he died, cried out, 'Let my cause be pleaded before the king!' That is the implied meaning of the statement in Genesis, 'The voice of your brother's blood cries out against Me.' "

In this circumspect way, the Midrash challenges even God's justice.

Midrash teaches us how to relate to other people. It is natural to rejoice at the downfall of our enemies. When the Israelites crossed the Sea of Reeds into freedom, the Bible relates that they broke into song. The Midrash says that the angels joined in that song but were silenced by God, exclaiming, "The work of My hands is drowning in the sea, and you desire to sing songs!" In fact, every Passover we are reminded of this midrashic lesson of compassion for all human beings—including our enemies—when we remove wine from our cups at the mention of each of the Ten Plagues.

Judaism has a universal message. The Torah is not solely the possession of the Jewish people; it is available to anyone wishing to study and practice it. This is the answer of the Midrash to the question of why the Torah was given in the wilderness of Sinai: "The Torah was given publicly and openly, in a place to which no one had any claim. For, if it had been given in the land of Israel, the nations of the world could have said: 'We can have no part of it.' Therefore it was given in the wilderness, publicly and openly, and in a place to which no one had any claim. Everyone who desires to accept it may come and accept it."

Throughout Jewish history, people who were not born Jewish have chosen to become Jews. Even in ancient times the rabbis were aware of people's propensity to be less than accepting of those who are different. They therefore laid down the precept of loving behavior toward Jews-by-Choice by telling this parable. (The rabbis often utilized parables as a teaching method.)

The Holy One, blessed be He, greatly loves the proselytes. To what may this be compared? To a king who had a flock which used to go out to the field and come in at evening.

So it was each day. Once a stag came in with the flock. He associated with the goats and grazed with them. When the flock came into the fold he came in with them; when they went out to graze he went out with them. The king was told: "A certain stag has joined the flock and is grazing with them every day. He goes out with them and comes in with them." The king felt an affection for him. When he went out into the field the king gave orders: "Let him have good pasture, such as he likes; no man shall beat him; be careful with him!" When he came in with the flock also the king would tell them: "Give him to drink"; and he loved him very much. The servants said to him: "Sovereign! You possess so many he-goats, you possess so many lambs, you possess so many kids, and you never caution us about them; yet you give us instructions every day about this stag!" Said the king to them: "The flock have no choice; whether they want or not, it is their nature to graze in the field all day and to come in at evening to sleep in the fold. The stags, however, sleep in the wilderness. It is not in their nature to come into places inhabited by people. Shall we then not account it as a merit to this one which has left behind the whole of the broad, vast wilderness, the abode of all the beasts, and has come to stay in the courtyard?" In like manner, ought we not to be grateful to proselytes who have left behind their people and all the other peoples of the world, and have chosen to come to us? Accordingly, God has provided them with special protection, for God exhorted Israel that they shall be very careful in relation to the proselytes so as not to do them harm.

Torah is seen as a gift from God—but as a gift with strings attached. Living by the Torah means following rules. The Midrash teaches that, before deciding to give this gift, God wanted some assurance that the people would really treasure it and live by it. The Israelites said, "Our ancestors will be our guarantors." God responded, "Your ancestors themselves require sureties! I have faults to find in your ancestors." The Israelites then offered the prophets as guarantors, but God found fault with them as well. Finally the Israelites offered their children as sureties. To this, God responded, "These are good guarantors; for their sake I will give you the Torah." This *midrash* underscores the role that children play in Jewish life. It also reflects the interrelatedness of the generations and the mutual responsibility of the generations in the continuation of Torah.

Continuity is a central theme in Judaism. Jewish tradition is seen as a chain, and each generation provides a new link. The concluding *midrash* of this chapter beautifully conveys the necessity of building for the future.

> A young man saw an old man planting a tree and taunted him, saying, "Old man, why are you planting that tree? You'll never live to see its fruits." The old man replied, "You may be right. I may never taste of its fruits. But this I know: 'As others before me planted trees so that I might eat, so I plant that future generations may enjoy the fruit of this tree.'"

Contemporary
Jewish Life

◆ ◆ ◆

MODERN MOVEMENTS
IN JUDAISM
JEWISH COMMUNITY

·21·

Modern Movements
in Judaism

North American Jews routinely identify themselves as Orthodox, Conservative, Reform, or Reconstructionist. (While this chapter focuses on the North American Jewish community, it is important to remember that the various movements are represented in other countries although sometimes called by different names). While these adjectives describe differences in approach to Jewish traditions, it is important to remember that they are only adjectives. Of course there are differences; however, more unites us than divides us. Jews share a common history and a common destiny. We are one people.

The movements in Jewish religious life are not denominations, but they do represent differing philosophies. We will give a brief overview of each of the movements and its beliefs. In practice, many Jews' religious observance cannot easily be pigeon-holed into a single particular movement. Within each movement, there is wide diversity in custom, practice, and observance, and regional differences also exist.

Orthodox

The movement most traditional in practice is known as Orthodox. The essential principle of Orthodox Judaism is *Torah min Hashamayim*, the Torah and all its commentaries and interpretations were divinely revealed. According to Orthodoxy, because all the laws and traditions were of direct divine origin, they must be followed by faithful Jews wishing to be loyal to God's will.

Orthodox Judaism espouses a *mitzvah*-centered life, with the *mitzvot* seen not as customs or folkways but as commandments from God. Both the ritual and ethical commandments are seen as equally binding. Therefore, the infraction of *any* commandment is considered a sin. Torah, not personal belief or conscience, is the arbiter of action.

Orthodox Judaism demands strict adherence to the laws governing every aspect of daily life. The dietary laws are scrupulously observed. A very traditional observance of the Sabbath, for instance, would include devoting the day to prayer, study, rest, and visiting with family and friends. Strict observance of *Shabbat* precludes riding, carrying, indeed engaging in any form of work. Orthodox services are conducted entirely in Hebrew, no musical instruments are used on *Shabbat* and major holidays, and men and women sit separately. The home is seen as the woman's domain while the synagogue is the man's. Women are not ordained as rabbis or counted in a *minyan,* nor are they permitted to lead worship services (with the exception of women's prayer groups, which some Orthodox authorities condone).

Orthodox Jews, by and large, strongly support Israel. However, some extreme right-wing Orthodox groups opposed the founding of Israel, believing that a Jewish commonwealth could be inaugurated only by the Messiah, and some continue a position of nonsupport.

Within the Orthodox community, there are gradations in observance and practice. The most traditional are known as Ultra-Orthodox; those that have made more accommodation with modernity are called Centrist or Modern Orthodox. The Ultra-Orthodox are extremely conservative in leading their lives. The men wear black hats, coats, and pants and white shirts, have untrimmed beards, and wear sidecurls (*payes*). The women dress very modestly and, if married, keep their heads covered.

Among the Ultra-Orthodox are the Chasidim, who follow the teachings of the eighteenth-century leader, Rabbi Israel, known as the Ba'al Shem Tov. At the time he lived, it was believed that the way to approach God was through study of Torah. He argued that God could also be approached by singing, dancing, fervent prayer, and even laughter. His philosophy spread very quickly throughout Eastern Europe. After his death, the chasidic movement divided into various groups, each with its own leader. Chasidism engendered a great deal of opposition among the mainstream religious leaders of the time. They were particularly opposed to the notion, which had developed, that the chasidic leader (*tzadik* or *rebbe*) was a wonder worker. While Chasidism began as a rather radical idea, over time it has come to be extremely conservative.

The Orthodox position is that theirs is the only legitimate approach to Judaism. The other movements are seen as deviations from authentic Torah-true Judaism.

Reform

The most liberal approach to Judaism is known as Reform (not Reformed). The Reform movement arose in Germany as a response to the challenges faced by the Jewish community as it entered the modern world. In the nineteenth century, Jews were increasingly allowed to enter into a society that had previously been forbidden to them. Many felt that the Judaism they had known was antiquated and not in keeping with the spirit of the modern age, and they sought to find a means to reconcile basic Jewish beliefs with life in the modern world.

The first reforms to be introduced were in the worship service. Prayers began to be offered in the vernacular as well as in Hebrew, and the service was shortened. While today weekly sermons are taken for granted, during the Middle Ages they were given only twice a year (on the *Shabbat* before *Pesach* and on the *Shabbat* between *Rosh Hashanah* and *Yom Kippur*). The Reformers insisted on a weekly sermon as a way of educating the community about the basic teachings of Judaism.

The essential principle of Reform is that religion is organic and dynamic. It must change to meet new situations. Reform has not shied away from innovating when changes were called for, nor has it feared to eliminate practices that it sees as outmoded. Some Reform innovations include the late Friday evening service (rather than a brief service at sundown), Confirmation, the seating of men and women together during services, and the use of musical instruments during *Shabbat* and holiday worship. Some of the practices that are generally no longer observed within Reform are prayers for the advent of a personal Messiah (today Reform Jews pray instead for the advent of a Messianic Age), prayers for the reestablishment of the ancient Temple sacrificial worship, and the practice of married women ritually immersing themselves after their menstrual period.

The Reform movement encourages individuals to study and make personal decisions concerning their religious practice. In making their determinations, the following criteria may be applied: Is this ceremony meaningful to me? Does it teach an ethical lesson? Is it aesthetically pleasing? Does it connect me more closely with the Jewish people and Jewish history?

One of the reasons Reform has been free to make changes is its belief that not every word in the Torah and its commentaries comes directly from God. Rather, the Torah is seen as a record of the encounter between the Jewish people and God. Torah is viewed as our reaching *toward* God rather than God commanding us. We might say that "Torah *contains* the word of God" rather than "it *is* the word of God." Reform places major emphasis on the autonomy of the individual and the absolute right to follow one's conscience.

While ritual has an important role to play in religious life, Reform insists that the essence of Judaism is its ethical teachings. It is not surprising, therefore, that the Reform movement has been in the forefront of all the struggles for human rights and that social action is at the top of the movement's agenda.

Reform Judaism has always been committed to the equality of the sexes in Jewish life. Boys and girls have always received the same education. Women are counted towards a *minyan* and have been in leadership positions in synagogues for many years. Reform was the first movement to ordain women as rabbis and to invest them as cantors.

The Reform movement, being open to change, has in fact changed its positions on several matters. In an earlier period, most Reform Jews did not favor the establishment of a Jewish state and did not observe the dietary laws. Men worshiped without wearing head coverings or prayer shawls, and the use of Hebrew at services was minimal. Today, the Reform movement is staunchly pro-Israel, and Hebrew is taught as a living language as well as for use during services. In many Reform temples, the wearing of *yarmulke* and *talit* is becoming more common, and many Reform Jews observe some level of *kashrut*.

Conservative

The Conservative movement began as a response to what its founders saw as the excesses of early Reform. They felt that the Reformers had given up too much of Jewish tradition, and they sought to find a middle ground whereby more of Judaism could be conserved. At the same time, they addressed the very same concern that Reform faced: how to adapt Judaism for its encounter with the modern world. Along with the early Reformers, they believed that the Orthodox approach was too rigid.

The Conservative movement maintains that Jewish law was not set for all time at Sinai but that the law has evolved over the course of Jewish history. While the individual is free to reject aspects of Jewish tradition, the movement regards Jewish law as binding and divinely inspired.

The movement is conservative in that changes are made slowly. Questions that pertain to the application of Jewish law in new situations are decided by a special rabbinical committee on law and standards. The movement upholds Sabbath observance and the dietary laws as standards.

The Conservative movement emphasizes attachment to the total worldwide Jewish community. Its educational programs focus on Jewish art, music, dance, literature, and modern Hebrew as well as classical Jewish studies.

Conservative services are rather traditional. Most of the service is in Hebrew although some of the prayers are recited in the vernacular.

The concept of Jewish peoplehood is very important in Conservative Judaism. While there is certainly concern for the betterment of society, on the whole the tone of Conservative Judaism is less universalistic than that of Reform.

Girls are given the same education as boys in Conservative schools. The question of whether women can be counted in the *minyan* or called to the Torah is decided by each synagogue. The Conservative movement has just begun to ordain women as rabbis over the objection of the more traditional elements of the movement.

Reconstructionist

The newest of the movements is Reconstructionism. This movement follows the teachings of Mordecai M. Kaplan. Kaplan taught that Judaism is more than a religion; it is an evolving religious civilization. Tradition, laws, customs, languages, literature, music, and art all combine to form what is called Judaism.

Israel is central to Reconstructionism. The symbol of the movement is a wheel—of which Zionism is the hub; religion, culture, and ethics are the spokes; and the Diaspora is the rim.

Reconstructionism rejects the notion that Jews are the chosen people. It also rejects the hope for the restoration of the ancient Jerusalem

Temple and has replaced a belief in a personal Messiah with a hope for the advent of a Messianic Era.

The real distinctiveness of Reconstructionism is in its theology. Kaplan presented a nonsupernatural God concept in which God is understood as the Process or Power that makes for salvation. God can be seen as the expression of the highest values, ideals, and virtues of the group. One Reconstructionist thinker, Harold Schulweis, speaks of Predicate Theology in which "God is love" is taken to mean "love is godly."

Since Reconstructionists do not believe in a supernatural God, the Torah is not seen as revealed truth. Rather it is seen as a reflection of the Jews' search for God.

Reconstructionist services are quite similar to Conservative services. They are somewhat traditional though they may include some creative readings as well.

Reconstructionism believes in full equality for men and women in Jewish life. It was this movement that developed the *Bat Mitzvah* ceremony, and the Reconstructionists ordain women as rabbis as well as count women toward a *minyan*.

In this chapter, we have attempted to present in a simple way something that is really quite complex. At times, it seems as if the religious movements defy characterization. There is often a good deal of overlap. The fact that there are different movements is seen by some as evidence of disunity. However, different types of synagogues meet the varying religious needs of the Jewish community. We believe that the variety of movements attests to the vitality and health of the North American Jewish community.

·22·

Jewish Community

Some two thousand years ago Hillel taught: "Do not separate yourself from the community." To be Jewish is not simply a matter of religious faith; it is to be part of a community. Jews are a religio-ethnic group, and Judaism comprises language, literature, law, and custom as well as religion. The concept of peoplehood has been present from the very foundation of Judaism. Indeed the three pillars of the Jewish religion are God, Torah, and the Jewish people.

The Concept of Community

Contemporary Jews exist on a historical continuum that stretches back to biblical times and comprises not only historical events but also a long collective memory. Thus, individual Jews view themselves as links in a chain of tradition, and they do not want that chain to be broken. This sense of shared history, values, and purpose creates a connection between Jews and Jewish communities throughout the world. Though Jews from different lands may have diverse backgrounds and experiences, they feel that there is a bond among them. The feeling among Jews can be described as that which exists in an extended family.

Every Jewish community is different, each having its own peculiar characteristics. Some are small, with a limited Jewish population and

Exterior of Touro Synagogue, Newport, Rhode Island, U.S.A. Photography by John T. Hopf.

all activities centering around the synagogue. Larger communities are more diverse, with a great variety of Jewish organizations and activities.

The Role of the Synagogue

The chief institution of Jewish life is the synagogue. Synagogues provide religious, educational, cultural, and social programs for the community. Jewish communities that are mid-sized or larger will generally have more than one congregation.

For thousands of years, the synagogue has served as a house of worship and much more. It has been and remains a place for both children and adults to learn about Judaism. For youngsters, this education takes place formally in religious school classes and informally in youth groups. Some youth movements are synagogue-related while others are run by other Jewish organizations. The synagogue is also a meeting place for the community. Whether used for a wedding reception, a temple committee meeting, or a planning session of a Jewish organization, the synagogue is a second home for Jews. Regardless of other Jewish groups to which Jews may belong, the synagogue remains the primary means of Jewish connectedness.

Synagogues, usually staffed by trained professionals, offer a variety of programs and services. While many of these are provided to the community at large, the temple depends upon its membership to sustain

Interior of Touro Synagogue, Newport, Rhode Island, U.S.A. Photography by John T. Hopf.

its activities. Membership in a synagogue entails making an annual financial commitment, commonly referred to as "dues." However, membership in a congregation is open to all, regardless of their financial status.

While it is clear that the rabbi is the religious leader of the synagogue, he or she is much more than that. The rabbi touches people's lives in many ways. The rabbi conducts the ceremonies that mark peak moments in the lives of individuals and families, such as baby namings, *Bar/Bat Mitzvah* ceremonies, weddings, and funerals. More than that, the rabbi is available for counsel and advice in times of difficulty, offering guidance and the perspective of Jewish tradition. Unlike the practice in olden times when rabbis often made their living in some business, craft, or occupation, modern rabbis, with larger congregations and far more duties and functions, are nearly always full-time rabbis, earning their living in this capacity.

While the Temple in ancient Jerusalem stood, it was central to Jewish religious life. The destruction of the Temple in the year 70 and the subsequent dispersion of the Jews could have meant the end of Jewish religious life and even the end of the Jewish people. That it didn't is due largely to the fact that the Jews found a way to carry Judaism with them wherever they went. That way was the synagogue, which has kept the message of Judaism alive through the centuries. Just as the synagogue kept the Jewish people alive in ancient times and throughout our wanderings, so the synagogue nourishes and sustains the Jewish people today.

Synagogue practices vary widely. There are differences associated with the Orthodox, Conservative, Reform, and Reconstructionist movements (see chapter on "Modern Movements in Judaism"). In addition to the differences among these religious movements, there are other diversities in religious practice that ought to be noted.

Ashkenazic and Sephardic Customs

Jews who lived in different parts of the world developed different customs. Jews who lived in Central and Eastern Europe and their descendants are known as *Ashkenazim* (the Hebrew word *Ashkenaz* means "Germany"). Jews who lived in Spain and Portugal and their descendants are known as *Sephardim* (the Hebrew word *Sepharad* means "Spain"). Jews whose origins are the Mediterranean Basin and the Middle East are generally grouped with the *Sephardim*.

For both the *Sephardim* and the *Ashkenazim,* Hebrew is the liturgical language. However, their pronunciation of Hebrew varies somewhat. For instance, the Hebrew word for the Sabbath is *Shabbos* in the Ashkenazic pronunciation and *Shabbat* in the Sephardic pronunciation. Since Israel has adopted the Sephardic pronunciation, that pronunciation is used by leaders of services in most North American synagogues. However, it is common to hear both pronunciations spoken by different worshipers in the same synagogue.

In addition to differences in Hebrew pronunciation, each group developed a folk language. For the *Ashkenazim,* it was Yiddish (related to German) while the *Sephardim* developed Ladino (related to Spanish). Sacred objects within the synagogue are sometimes called by different names. For example, *Ashkenazim* call the Holy Ark the *Aron Hakodesh* while *Sephardim* call it the *Heichal;* the raised platform from which the Torah scroll is read is known as the *bimah* in Ashkenazic synagogues and as the *tevah* in Sephardic synagogues.

The cuisine of each group developed along the lines of the countries in which the Jews lived. While Jews traditionally eat dairy foods on *Shavuot, Ashkenazim* eat *blintzes* and *Sephardim* eat cheese-filled pastries. Though the specific foods differ, the cuisines do follow the Jewish dietary laws.

Probably the most divergent custom between *Ashkenazim* and *Sephardim* concerns the naming of children. Among Ashkenazic Jews, babies are named in memory of a deceased relative and not in honor of anyone living. *Sephardim* customarily name children in honor of a living relative, particularly a grandparent. Thus the different customs between Ashkenazic and Sephardic Jews can be seen in personal life as well as in the synagogue.

The Nature of the Community

In larger Jewish communities there are a number of businesses catering to Jewish needs. Among these may be kosher butchers, Jewish bakeries, and delicatessens. Jewish bookstores often also sell religious articles such as *mezuzot, menorot,* and *Shabbat* candlesticks. Most synagogues also have gift shops selling these types of objects.

Jewish culture can be appreciated in a number of settings. Jewish museums are found in many large cities; some synagogues also have interesting collections of Judaica. The museums sponsor cultural and educational programing in addition to their changing exhibits. Jewish community forums and Jewish community centers often bring in guest lecturers and music, theater, or dance troupes. In the larger communities there are institutions of higher Jewish learning sponsoring adult education programs. Support groups for Israeli universities, hospitals, museums, and social service institutions are active throughout North America.

There are also a number of service organizations providing support for a variety of institutions while, at the same time, creating educational and social programs for their members. Some of these are temple sisterhoods and brotherhoods, ORT, Hadassah, the National Council of Jewish Women, and B'nai B'rith. Several groups are engaged in the battle against bigotry and prejudice, including anti-Semitism. Among them are the American Jewish Committee, the American Jewish Congress, and the Anti-Defamation League of B'nai B'rith.

Most Jewish communities have a Federation serving as the umbrella organization for many diverse agencies and groups. Federations raise money for the United Jewish Appeal, which is the major conduit of funds to Israel's social welfare programs. Federations also support such local agencies as the Jewish Family Service, the Bureau of Jewish Education, and the Jewish Home for the Aging. While we may contribute time and money to our own favorite charities, we recognize—in addition—that we have an obligation to support the total Jewish community. An annual pledge to the Federation campaign is seen as a self-imposed tax whereby we fulfill our commitment to sustaining Jewish life and enabling the community to function smoothly.

While the various Jewish organizations are professionally staffed, almost all of them rely on volunteers to promote and support their work. The Midrash teaches: "A community is too heavy for any one person to carry alone." The community is strengthened by individual involvement, and, in turn, individuals derive greater satisfaction as community members by their active participation.

Afterword

At the beginning of this book, we said, "Go and study!" You have just taken an important step on what we hope will be a lifelong journey on the path of Jewish learning.

There is much that is not within these pages. No single book could possibly encompass the richness and depth of Judaism. We hope that we have whetted your appetite to learn more and that you will now take the next step. Choose some books from the bibliography. Visit your local Jewish library or bookstore. Seek out other opportunities, both formal and informal, for learning.

In the prayers of the morning service, we say:

> . . . guide us to know and understand, learn and teach, observe and uphold with love all the teachings of Your Torah.

This is our prayer for you, dear reader.

Glossary

Afikoman: A Greek word meaning "dessert." This piece of the ceremonial *matzah* is the final thing eaten at the Passover *seder* meal.

Al Chet: Literally: for the sin; an important *Yom Kippur* prayer listing sins for which we beg forgiveness.

Aliyah: Literally: going up. To "have an *aliyah*" refers to the honor of being called up to the *bimah* to recite or chant the blessings over the Torah. To "make *aliyah*" or "go on *aliyah*" means to immigrate to Israel.

Ani Ma'amin: Literally: I believe; often sung at the *seder* and at *Yom Hashoah* observances in memory of Holocaust victims who sang this song of faith on their way to their deaths.

Apocrypha: A collection of religious writings not included in the Hebrew Scriptures.

Arba'ah Minim: See the Four Species.

Aron Hakodesh: Literally: the Holy Ark; the special cabinet in which the Torah scrolls are kept in the synagogue; the Holy Ark is called *Heichal* in Sephardic synagogues.

Ashkenazi(c): Referring to Jews of Central and Eastern European origin.

Ashkenazim: Jews of Central and Eastern European background.

Aufruf: Calling up of the bridegroom or bridal couple for the Torah blessings on the *Shabbat* preceding their wedding.

Avinu Malkenu: Literally: our Father, our King; a prayer of supplication recited on *Yom Kippur*.

Badeken: Traditional formal veiling of the bride by the groom before the wedding ceremony.

Bar/Bat (Bas) Mitzvah: Literally: son/daughter of the commandment; ceremony marking a youngster's reaching the age of religious majority, traditionally thirteen for boys and twelve for girls; in many congregations, thirteen for girls as well.

Berachah (pl., **Berachot**):   Blessing.

Berit, B'ris: Literally: covenant; refers to the covenant between God and Abraham and his descendants. The ceremony of *Berit Milah* is often referred to simply as *b'ris.*

Berit Habat: Literally: Covenant for a (newborn) Daughter; name for a home naming ceremony of baby girls.

Berit Hachayim: Literally: Covenant of Life; another name for *Berit Habat.*

Berit Milah: Literally: Covenant of Circumcision; traditionally performed on the eighth day of a boy's life.

Bet Din: Rabbinical court.

Bimah: The raised platform in the synagogue from which the Torah is read and from which worship services are usually conducted (in Ashkenazic congregations); the platform is called *tevah* in Sephardic synagogues.

Birkat Hamazon: Grace after meals.

Blintzes: Crêpes filled with cheese or fruit, traditionally eaten on *Shavuot.*

Chag Habikurim: Literally: Festival of the First Fruits; another name for *Shavuot,* one of the three Pilgrimage Festivals.

Chag Sameach: Literally: a joyous holiday; greeting used on the festivals.

Chai: Literally: life. When Jews drink, we wish each other *Lechayim* (to life).

Chalah (pl., **Chalot**):   Egg bread eaten on *Shabbat* and festivals; the *chalah* used on *Rosh Hashanah* is round, often containing raisins, symbolizing a sweet year, distinguishing it from the *Shabbat chalah* that is braided.

Chamets: Leavened bread and anything made with wheat, rye, barley, oats, or spelt, which has not been supervised to ensure that it has not leavened; refers to prohibited foods during *Pesach.*

Chanukah: Literally: dedication; name of the winter holiday commemorating the Maccabean victory over the Syrians in 165 B.C.E.

Chanukat Habayit: Literally: dedication of the home; the ceremony of affixing the *mezuzah.*

Chanukiah: Eight-branched candelabrum, with a place for a ninth candle (*shamash*) that lights the others, especially designed for *Chanukah*.

Charoset: A mixture of fruits, nuts, and wine; one of the symbolic Passover foods. Its color and consistency are reminders of the bricks and mortar used by the Israelite slaves.

Chasidim: Ultra-Orthodox followers of the eighteenth-century leader, Rabbi Israel, the Ba'al Shem Tov.

Chatan: Bridegroom.

Chatan Bereshit: Literally: bridegroom of Genesis; the man called to recite or chant the blessings over the first section of the Torah on *Simchat Torah*.

Chatan Torah: Literally: bridegroom of the Torah; the man called to recite or chant the blessings over the final section of the Torah on *Simchat Torah*.

Chavurah (pl., **Chavurot**):   Informal group, which meets together for Jewish study and celebration.

Chazan: A cantor.

Cheder: Old-fashioned term for Hebrew school.

Chet: Literally: missing the mark; one of the Hebrew terms translated as sin.

Chevrah Kadisha: Group of people entrusted with the *mitzvah* of preparing a body for burial.

Chupah: Wedding canopy; it can be a *talit* or a velvet or silk canopy or a floral bower.

Confirmation: Ceremony marking the completion of the religious school course of study, often held on *Shavuot*.

Consecration: Ceremony marking the beginning of a child's formal Jewish education, often held on *Simchat Torah*.

Cup of Elijah: A wine goblet set aside for the prophet Elijah at the *seder* table; Elijah is the proverbial herald of the Messianic Era when justice and peace will be realized.

Daven: The Yiddish word meaning "pray."

Dayenu: Literally: It would have been enough for us; name of a popular *seder* song.

Devar Torah: Literally: a word of Torah; follows the Torah reading in a worship service, taking the form of a sermon, talk, explication, story, discussion, or program.

Diaspora: Jewish communities outside of Israel.

Dreidel: Yiddish term for a four-sided top, used in a *Chanukah* game. In Hebrew, the top is known as a *sevivon*.

Echah: Hebrew name for the biblical Book of Lamentations; is read on *Tishah Be'av.*

El Malei Rachamim: Literally: God, full of compassion; memorial prayer.

Erusin: In ancient times, the formal engagement ceremony before marriage.

Etrog: Citron; with the *lulav,* it is the symbol of *Sukot.*

Federation: The central coordinating agency of the Jewish community.

Fleishig: Foods derived from meat or meat products.

The Four Questions: Questions asked at the *seder.* The answers to these questions form the rest of the *haggadah.*

The Four Species (Arba'ah Minim): Palm, myrtle, willow, and citron; another name for the *lulav* and *etrog* together, used on *Sukot.*

Gan Eden: Literally: Garden of Eden; paradise.

Gefilte Fish: A mixture of chopped fish and seasonings which is poached and served cold with horseradish; a traditional Ashkenazic food.

Gehinnom: Literally: Valley of Hinnom; a temporary place of punishment in the afterlife.

Gelt: Yiddish term for money; traditionally given as a *Chanukah* gift and used for the *dreidel* game.

Gemar Chatimah Tovah: Literally: May the final sealing be good; traditional greeting from the end of *Rosh Hashanah* through *Yom Kippur.*

Gemara: Collection of legal and ethical discussions of the rabbis of the third through the fifth centuries, edited about 500 C.E.; together with the *Mishnah* forms the Talmud.

Gematria: Hebrew numerology.

Ger/Gioret: The masculine and feminine forms of the Hebrew term for convert.

Gerut: The process of conversion.

Get: Religious divorce; the word is used to refer to a Jewish bill of divorcement.

Ghetto: Walled-off section of a city where Jews were forced to live.

Grogger: Noisemaker used to drown out Haman's name during the reading of the *Megillah* on *Purim;* these noisemakers are sometimes called *greggers* or *graggers.*

Gut Shabbos: Literally: good Sabbath; a Yiddish Sabbath greeting. Some people anglicize this to "Good *Shabbos.*"

Gut Yontif: Literally: a good holiday; a Yiddish greeting used on all festivals.

Hachnasat Orechim: Hospitality.

Haftarah: Selection from the Prophets read or chanted after the weekly Torah portion during the synagogue service on Sabbath and holidays.

Haggadah (pl., **Haggadot**):   Literally: telling; book in which the Passover story is retold and the *seder* ritual is outlined. It is our duty to tell the story of Passover, particularly to the children.

Hakafah (pl., **Hakafot**):   The carrying of the Torah scrolls in a procession around the sanctuary.

Halachah: Jewish law.

Hallel: Special psalms of praise, recited or sung on the festivals.

Hamantashen: Filled three-cornered pastries supposed to represent Haman's hat, traditionally eaten on *Purim.*

Harei at mekudeshet li betaba'at zo kedat Mosheh veyisrael: Literally: Behold you are consecrated unto me, with this ring, according to the law of Moses and Israel; this is the Hebrew nuptial formula.

Hatafat Dam Berit: Taking a single drop of blood from the penis as a sign of the covenant, necessary in the conversion of an adult male already circumcised.

Havdalah: Literally: separation; ceremony that marks the end of the Sabbath and the beginning of the week.

Hebrew School: Midweek afternoon Hebrew classes.

Hechag: Literally: the holiday; one of the names for *Sukot.*

High Holy Days: *Rosh Hashanah* and *Yom Kippur;* also called, the High Holidays or, simply, the Holidays.

Kabbalat Ol Mitzvot: Literally: the acceptance of the yoke of the commandments; a convert's agreement to lead a Jewish life.

Kabbalat Shabbat: Psalms, readings, and songs welcoming the Sabbath; the introductory portion of the Sabbath eve service.

Kaddish: Prayer praising God. This prayer is chanted at several points in a service. In addition, it is recited at least once at each service in memory of those who have died.

Kalah: Bride.

Kalat Bereshit: Literally: bride of Genesis; the woman called to recite or chant the blessings over the first section of the Torah on *Simchat Torah*.

Kalat Torah: Literally: bride of the Torah; the woman called to recite or chant the blessings over the final section of the Torah on *Simchat Torah*.

Kallah (pl., **Kallot**): Conclave or retreat.

Karpas: A green herb like parsley or a green vegetable such as celery or watercress, symbolizing spring; one of the symbolic foods used on the *seder* plate.

Kashrut: Jewish dietary laws.

Kavanah: Literally: intentionality; referring to the spiritual attitude with which we approach worship.

Ken Ayin Hara (Yiddish, **Kinna Hurra**): Literally: May there be no evil eye.

Keriah: Tearing of a garment or a symbolic black ribbon as an expression of grief in conjunction with a death.

Ketubah (pl., **Ketubot**): Marriage contract.

Ketuvim: Literally: the Writings; third section of the Bible.

Kevah: Literally: fixed; referring to the fixed order of Jewish liturgy.

Kevod Hamet: Honor due to the dead.

Kiddush: Blessing recited or chanted over wine on *Shabbat* or festivals emphasizing their holiness.

Kiddush Cup: Ceremonial wine cup used for *Kiddush*.

Kiddush Pe'ter Rechem: Modern ceremony celebrating the birth of a first child.

Kiddushin: Literally: holiness; refers both to the wedding ceremony and to the state of matrimony.

Kipah: The Hebrew term for skullcap; the Yiddish term is *yarmulke*.

Kittel: White garment that is part of traditional Jewish burial clothes; worn by some worshipers on *Yom Kippur* as a reminder of mortality and a symbol of purity, and by some officiants at *Rosh Hashanah* services and at the Passover *seder*. Also worn by some grooms at their wedding.

Klaf: Hand-written scroll placed in a *mezuzah*, containing Deuteronomy 6:4–9; 11:13–21.

Kodesh: Literally: holy.

Kohelet: Hebrew name for the biblical Book of Ecclesiastes; it is read on *Sukot*.

Kohen (pl., **Kohanim**):   Descendant of the ancient priestly class, the progeny of Aaron.

Kol Nidrei: Literally: all vows; prayer that begins the *Yom Kippur* eve service; the entire service is often called the *Kol Nidrei* service.

Kosher: Ritually fit for use.

Kugel: Baked noodle or potato pudding.

Kvatter/Kvatterin: Godfather/Godmother; those who carry the baby into the *Berit* ceremony.

Ladino: Judeo-Spanish; the everyday language of Sephardic Jews.

Latke (pl., **Latkes**):   Yiddish word for pancake; traditionally, potato *latkes* are eaten on *Chanukah* and *matzah* meal *latkes* on Passover.

Lehitpalel: Literally: to judge oneself; the Hebrew word meaning "to pray."

Leshanah Tovah Tikatevu: Literally: May you be inscribed [in the Book of Life] for a good year; *Rosh Hashanah* greeting, sometimes shortened to *Shanah Tovah*.

Levivot: Hebrew term for potato *latkes*.

Lulav: Palm branch, with myrtle and willow sprigs attached; with the *etrog,* it is the symbol of *Sukot*.

Machzor: High Holy Day prayer book. In some Orthodox synagogues, a special prayer book—also known as a *machzor*—is used on the Pilgrimage Festivals.

Mamaloshen: Literally: mother language; affectionate term for Yiddish.

Maot Chitim: Literally: wheat money; money collected prior to Passover to assist the needy to celebrate the holiday and to buy special Passover foods.

Maoz Tsur: Best-known *Chanukah* song. An English version of the song is entitled "Rock of Ages."

Maror: A bitter herb such as horseradish, symbolizing the bitter plight of the enslaved Israelites; one of the symbolic foods used on the *seder* plate.

Marranos: Jews, in Spain and Portugal, who were forcibly converted to Christianity but practiced Judaism secretly.

Mashiach: See Messiah.

Matzah (pl., **Matzot**): The unleavened bread eaten in recollection of the hurried departure from Egypt; the eating of *matzah* is obligatory only at the *seder*. During the rest of *Pesach,* while one must avoid all *chamets,* one may also abstain from *matzah.*

Mazal Tov: Literally: good luck; congratulations.

Megillah (pl., **Megillot**): Literally: scroll; there are five *megillot* in the Bible. The one we read on *Sukot* is Ecclesiastes (*Kohelet*), on *Purim* we read Esther (*Ester*), on *Pesach* we read Song of Songs (*Shir Hashirim*), on *Shavuot* we read Ruth (*Rut*), and on *Tishah Be'av* (a fast day on the ninth of *Av* commemorating the destruction of the First and Second Temples in Jerusalem), we read Lamentations (*Echah*).

Menorah (pl., **Menorot**): Seven- or eight-branched candelabrum; people commonly refer to an eight-branched *Chanukiah* as a *menorah.*

Mentsh: A caring, concerned, decent, principled human being. Calling a man or a woman a *mentsh* is the highest possible compliment.

Messiah (Mashiach): Literally: the anointed one; the flesh-and-blood king who traditionally is expected to establish Jewish independence in our own land and usher in the era of universal peace.

Mezuzah (pl., **Mezuzot**): Ritual object consisting of a casing and a *klaf* (scroll) that is put on the doorpost(s) of the house.

Midrash (pl., **Midrashim**): The Midrash is a collection of works compiled between the third and twelfth centuries that seeks out underlying truths and meanings of the Bible; the result of the process of delving into the ramifications of a biblical verse and of the ancient rabbis' reading between the lines of Scripture.

Mikdash Me'at: Literally: a small sanctuary; refers to the home.

Mikveh: Ritual bath. The *mikveh* is traditionally used by a bride prior to her wedding and by women after their monthly menstruation and after childbirth. Immersion in a *mikveh* is one of the traditional requirements of conversion for both men and women. The *mikveh* may be used by men as a spiritual preparation for Sabbaths, festivals, and holy days.

Milchig: Dairy foods or dairy products.

Minyan: Quorum of ten adult Jews necessary for public prayer. In Orthodox and some Conservative synagogues, only men can constitute a *minyan*. In other Conservative synagogues as well as in all Reform and Reconstructionist congregations, men and women count toward the *minyan*.

Mi Sheberach: Literally: May the One who blessed . . . ; a prayer usually, but not solely, recited after a person has been honored with a Torah blessing. There are various forms of this prayer, one of which is used to name a child and another to pray for the recovery of a sick person.

Mishlei: Hebrew name for the biblical Book of Proverbs.

Mishlo'ach Manot: Sending portions of food to friends to celebrate *Purim;* also referred to as *Shalach Monos.*

Mishnah: Code of Jewish law edited by Rabbi Judah Ha-Nasi about 200 C.E.; together with the *Gemara* forms the Talmud.

Mitzvah (pl., Mitzvot): Literally: commandment; a religious precept or obligation; *mitzvah* refers to one of the 613 commandments in the Torah. Broadly interpreted, a *mitzvah* is the response of Jews to what they believe the Torah expects of them as members of a covenant-community.

Mohel (pl., Mohalim): Highly skilled ritual circumciser.

Motzi: Literally: [God] who brings forth [bread]; blessing over bread; standard blessing before meals at which bread is served.

Names of God: *Adonai, Elohim, El Shaddai, YHVH, Hakadosh Baruch Hu, Ribono shel Olam, Harachaman, Avinu Shebashamayim.*

Neilah: Literally: closing; concluding service of *Yom Kippur.*

Nevi'im: Literally: the Prophets; second section of the Bible.

Nisuin: In ancient times, the formal wedding ceremony.

Olam Haba: Literally: the world-to-come; refers to the life of the soul after death.

Oneg Shabbat: Literally: joy of the Sabbath; reception after Friday night services, which includes refreshments, socializing, and, sometimes, Israeli dancing or a discussion.

Parashah: The weekly Torah portion; also called *sidrah* or *sedrah.*

Pareve: Foods containing neither meat/meat derivatives nor milk/milk derivatives and which according to the Jewish dietary laws may be eaten with either milk or meat meals (e.g., fruits, vegetables, eggs, fish).

Payes: Sidecurls worn by Ultra-Orthodox men and boys.

Pesach: Passover; the festival commemorating the Exodus from Egypt as related in the Book of Exodus; one of the three Pilgrimage Festivals.

Pidyon Haben/Habat: Literally: redemption of the (firstborn) son/daughter; home ceremony that takes place on the thirty-first day of a child's life.

Pilgrimage Festivals: *Sukot, Pesach,* and *Shavuot;* the three harvest festivals commanded by the Torah on which our ancestors made a pilgrimage to the Temple to make a festival offering.

Pogrom: Russian word meaning an organized attack on the Jewish community.

Purim: Literally: lots; festival that celebrates the survival of the Jewish people. The commandment to celebrate this festival is found in the Book of Esther.

Purimspiel: Humorous play put on at *Purim.*

Pushke: Yiddish for *tsedakah* box; container for coins given to charitable causes.

Refusenik: A Jew who has been refused permission by the government to emigrate from the Soviet Union.

Religious School: Synagogue-related school where children receive Jewish education in afternoon and weekend classes.

Rosh Hashanah: Literally: head of the year; the Jewish New Year festival.

Sandak: Person who holds the baby during the *Berit Milah* ceremony.

Seder: Literally: order; ritual for the home celebration of the first (and second) evening(s) of *Pesach.*

Sefer Torah: Torah scroll.

Selichot: Prayers for forgiveness.

Selichot Service: A service of preparation for the High Holy Days, usually held at midnight on the Saturday preceding Rosh Hashanah.

Sephardi(c):   Referring to Jews of Mediterranean origin.

Sephardim: Jews whose origin is in the Mediterranean Basin.

Seudah: Feast.

Seudah shel Mitzvah: A festive meal that honors the observance of a *mitzvah;* same as *Seudat Mitzvah.*

Seudah Shelishit: Literally: third meal; a light meal eaten late on *Shabbat* afternoon.

Seudat Havra'ah: Literally: meal of condolence; prepared by friends of the mourners and eaten in the house of mourning immediately following a funeral.

Seudat Mitzvah: See *Seudah shel Mitzvah*.

Sevivon: Hebrew term for *dreidel*.

Shabbat: The Sabbath (Sephardic pronunciation).

Shabbat Hagadol: Literally: the Great Sabbath; the Sabbath preceding Passover.

Shabbat Shalom: Literally: a Sabbath of peace; Hebrew Sabbath greeting.

Shabbat Shuvah: Literally: Sabbath of Return; the Sabbath between *Rosh Hashanah* and *Yom Kippur*. It gets its name from its *haftarah* that begins "*Shuvah Yisrael*" (Return, O Israel—Hosea 14:2).

Shabbat Zachor: The Sabbath immediately preceding *Purim;* its name is taken from the additional Torah portion read that day, Deuteronomy 25:17–19, that begins with the word "*Zachor*" (Remember).

Shabbaton (pl., Shabbatonim): A Sabbath program of study and celebration.

Shabbos: The Sabbath (Ashkenazic pronunciation); also used in Yiddish.

Shabbosdik: Having a Sabbath atmosphere.

Shalach Monos: See *Mishlo'ach Manot*.

Shamash: Literally: servant; term for the ninth candle used to light the other candles in the *Chanukiah*.

Shames: Yiddish term for *shamash*.

Shankbone: One of the symbols on the *seder* plate; the shankbone is symbolic of the ancient paschal sacrifice.

Shavuot: Literally: weeks; festival occuring seven weeks after the beginning of *Pesach;* one of the three Pilgrimage Festivals.

Shehecheyanu: Literally: [God] who has kept us alive; this is the blessing for beginnings and other happy occasions in people's lives, such as birth and marriage. It is also said at candlelighting, *Kiddush*, and certain other specific times during festival observances.

Shelom Bayit: Literally: peace in the home. Judaism encourages behavior that maintains or leads to a peaceful, harmonious atmosphere in the home.

Sheloshim: Thirty-day mourning period.

Shema: The main statement of Jewish belief: "*Shema Yisrael Adonai Elohenu Adonai Echad*" (Hear, O Israel: the Lord is our God, the Lord is One).

Shemini Atseret: Literally: the eighth day of assembly; conclusion of *Sukot*.

Sheol: A word used in the Bible to describe the afterlife; the netherworld.

Sheva Berachot: Literally: seven blessings; these are recited or chanted at a wedding ceremony prior to the sharing of a cup of wine by the bride and groom.

Shir Hashirim: Hebrew name for the biblical book of Song of Songs; it is read on *Pesach*.

Shivah: Seven-day mourning period, the first day of which is the day of burial.

Shochet: Ritual slaughterer, required by Jewish dietary laws for the preparation of kosher meat.

Shofar: Ram's horn; instrument blown on *Rosh Hashanah* as a call to conscience and at the end of *Yom Kippur* to draw the High Holy Days to a close.

Shomer: Literally: guardian; person who remains with the deceased so that the body is never left alone prior to burial.

Shtetl (pl., **Shtetlach**): A small Jewish village in Eastern Europe.

Shuckle: To sway during prayer.

Shul: The Yiddish term for synagogue.

Siddur: Prayer book.

Sidrah or Sedrah: See *Parashah*.

Simchah: Literally: joy; a happy event.

Simchat Torah: Literally: joy of the Torah; holiday marking the conclusion of the yearly cycle of Torah readings and the beginning of the new cycle; the final fall holiday.

Sofer: A specially trained scribe.

Sufganiot: Jelly doughnuts, served in Israel on *Chanukah*.

Sukah (pl., **Sukot**): Booth, hut, or tabernacle covered with branches and decorated with hanging fruits, vegetables, and other decorations, built in observance of the festival of *Sukot*.

Sukot: Literally: booths; name of the festival that commemorates the Israelites' wanderings in the desert after leaving Egypt and before entering the Promised Land; one of the three Pilgrimage Festivals.

Sunday School: Weekend classes of religious schools.

Tachrichim: Burial shrouds.

Taharah: Ritual purification of the deceased in preparation for burial.

Talit (Talis): Prayer shawl.

Talmud: Comprised of both the *Mishnah* and *Gemara,* the Talmud is the collected legal and ethical discussions of the rabbis, edited around the year 500 C.E.

TaNaCH: Way of referring to the Bible using the acronym for *Torah* (Five Books of Moses), *Nevi'im* (Prophets) and *Ketuvim* (Writings); the three sections of the Hebrew Bible.

Tashlich: Traditional *Rosh Hashanah* afternoon ceremony in which individuals symbolically cast their sins into a body of water.

Tefilah: Literally: prayer; also refers to the central group of prayers in each service, alternatively called the *Amidah* or *Shemoneh Esreh.*

Tefilin: Prayer boxes worn during weekday morning worship.

Teshuvah: Literally: turning or returning; a Hebrew term for repentance.

Tevilah: Literally: immersion. This can take place in any natural body of water or in a specially constructed ritual bath known as a *mikveh.*

Tikkun Leil Shavuot: Literally: service of the night of *Shavuot;* an anthology of selections from the Bible, the *Mishnah,* and mystical works used for the all-night study session on *Shavuot.*

Tikkun Olam: Repairing our broken world; the concept in Judaism that Jews, as part of the human family, have a responsibility to contribute to the well-being of the broken world, thereby repairing it.

Tishah Be'av: The ninth day of the month of *Av;* a day of mourning for the destruction of the ancient Temple in Jerusalem.

Torah: Literally: teaching; in its most narrow sense, it is the first section (the Five Books of Moses or Pentateuch) of the Bible, hand-written on a parchment scroll; in its broadest sense, it is all of Judaism, which flows from those books.

Torah min Hashamayim: The concept that the entire Torah is of direct divine origin.

Treif: Literally: torn apart; food that is not ritually fit. It is the opposite of kosher.

Tsedakah: Literally: justice or righteousness; the Hebrew word we use for charity and charitable acts. It is customary to give *tsedakah* prior to candlelighting in the home, in honor of a *simchah,* and in memory of a loved one.

Tsedakah Box: See *Pushke.*

Tsimmes: A sweet side dish, which is either baked or stewed, consisting of a variety of ingredients such as carrots, prunes, potatoes, and—sometimes—beef.

Tu Bishvat: Fifteenth day of the month of *Shevat;* a minor holiday known as the New Year of the Trees, observed by planting trees.

Ulpan (pl., **Ulpanim**): Intensive course preparing students to become proficient in modern spoken Hebrew.

Unveiling: Dedication of a grave marker, which can take place any time after *sheloshim.*

Ushpizin: Symbolic guests from Jewish history invited to a *sukah,* an example of hospitality.

Ve'ahavta: Literally: and you shall love; the prayer from Deuteronomy 6:5–9, that obligates us to love God and to teach Judaism to future generations; part of the *Shema.*

Yachats: The breaking of the middle *matzah* of the ceremonial *matzot* during a Passover *seder.*

Yad: Literally: hand; pointer used by Torah readers to keep their place while reading from the scroll.

Yad Vashem: A Holocaust memorial in Jerusalem.

Yahrzeit: Anniversary of a death.

Yahrzeit Candle: A twenty-four-hour memorial candle lit on the anniversary of a loved one's death (*yahrzeit*), as well as on those days when *Yizkor* is recited.

Yamim Noraim: Literally: the Days of Awe; the ten-day period beginning with *Rosh Hashanah* and ending with *Yom Kippur.*

Yarmulke: The Yiddish term for skullcap; the Hebrew term is *kipah.*

Yichud: Time spent alone together by the bride and groom immediately after the wedding ceremony.

Yiddish: Judeo-German; the everyday language of the Jews of Eastern Europe.

Yizkor: Memorial service recited on *Yom Kippur* as well as on the last day of *Sukot, Pesach* and *Shavuot.*

Yom Ha'atsmaut: Israel Independence Day.

Yom Hadin: Literally: Day of Judgment; one of the names for *Rosh Hashanah*.

Yom Hashoah: Holocaust Memorial Day.

Yom Hazikaron: Literally: Day of Remembrance; one of the names for *Rosh Hashanah*.

Yom Kippur: Literally: Day of Atonement; day of fasting and intense introspection, one of the High Holy Days.

Yom Tov: Hebrew term for holiday.

Yontif: Yiddish term for holiday.

Zeman Matan Toratenu: Literally: the Season of the Giving of Our Torah; another name for *Shavuot*, one of the three Pilgrimage Festivals.

Zeman Simchatenu: Literally: the Season of Our Joy; another name for *Sukot*, one of the three Pilgrimage Festivals.

Zichronah Livrachah: May her memory be a blessing.

Zichrono Livrachah: May his memory be a blessing.

Zionism: The belief that there should be a Jewish national homeland in the historic land of Israel.

Bibliography

This is a selective bibliography. A more extensive bibliography can be found in *Choosing Judaism,* by Lydia Kukoff (New York: Union of American Hebrew Congregations, 1981), pp. 132–150. Another extremely helpful bibliographic source is *The Book of Jewish Books,* by Ruth S. Frank and William Wollheim (New York: Harper and Row, 1986), which contains extensive annotated listings, by topic, of outstanding Jewish books.

Anti-Semitism
Reuther, Rosemary. *Faith and Fratricide.* Seabury Press, 1974.
   A brilliant study of the theological roots of anti-Semitism.

Sartre, Jean-Paul. *Anti-Semite and Jew.* Translated from the French by George J. Becker. Schocken, 1948.
   A brilliant portrait of both anti-Semite and Jew, written by a non-Jew from a non-Jewish point of view.

Bible
Cohen, A., ed. *The Soncino Books of the Bible.* Soncino Press, 1946–1984.
   This 14-volume set contains both the Hebrew text and the 1917 Jewish Publication Society English translation. Each book contains extensive selections from the classical Jewish commentators.

Hertz, J. H., ed. *The Pentateuch and Haftorahs.* Soncino Press, 1978.
   This volume contains both the Hebrew text and the 1917 Jewish Publication Society English translation. The commentaries include writings from ancient, medieval, and modern periods and reflect a traditional outlook.

Heschel, Abraham J. *The Prophets*. The Jewish Publication Society of America, 1962.

An outstanding description of the message of the biblical prophets.

Sandmel, Samuel. *The Enjoyment of Scripture: The Law, the Prophets, and the Writings*. Oxford University Press, 1974.

Concerned with the literary method and quality of the various kinds of writings found in the Holy Scriptures.

TaNaKH: A New Translation of the Holy Scriptures. The Jewish Publication Society of America, 1985.

A scholarly and readable English translation of the Holy Scriptures taking into account the latest linguistic researches and archeological discoveries.

The Torah: A Modern Commentary. Commentaries by W. Gunther Plaut and Bernard J. Bamberger, with essays on ancient Near Eastern literature by William W. Hallo. Union of American Hebrew Congregations, 1981.

This first major Reform commentary contains the Hebrew text, the 1962 Jewish Publication Society translation, incisive interpretations, and related writings from an encyclopedic range of sources. Also included are the *haftarot* for each *sidrah* and for special days.

Christianity and Judaism

Keeping Posted. Volume XIX, Number 3, December 1973, "Judaism and Christianity: The Parting of the Ways."

Sandmel, Samuel. *We Jews and Jesus*. Oxford University Press, 1973.

Written in a nontechnical style for the layperson, this book describes the what and why of the Jewish attitude to Jesus.

Silver, Abba Hillel. *Where Judaism Differed*. Macmillan, 1956.

A lively account of the distinctive values and outlook of Judaism and an exploration of the sharp divergencies between Judaism and Christianity.

Weiss-Rosmarin, Trude. *Judaism and Christianity: The Differences*. Jonathan David, 1965.

Concise, popular presentation of the teachings of and differences between Judaism and Christianity.

Food

Engle, Fannie, and Blair, Gertrude. *The Jewish Festival Cookbook*. Warner Paperback Library, 1954.
Recipes and menus for all the Jewish holidays as well as a description of holiday customs.

Gethers, Judith, and Lefft, Elizabeth. *The World-Famous Ratner's Meatless Cookbook*. Bantam Books, 1975.
Authentic recipes from Ratner's Dairy Restaurant in New York.

Greene, Gloria Kaufer. *The Jewish Holiday Cookbook*. Times Books, 1985.
These recipes are from both Ashkenazic and Sephardic traditions and are arranged by holiday.

Grossinger, Jennie. *The Art of Jewish Cooking*. Bantam Books, 1958.
Over 300 traditional recipes from an expert on Jewish cooking.

Nathan, Joan. *The Jewish Holiday Kitchen*. Schocken, 1979.
A presentation of the history, food requirements, and traditions of each of the Jewish holidays along with a collection of recipes.

Rockland, Mae S. *The Jewish Party Book: A Contemporary Guide to Customs, Crafts, and Foods*. Schocken, 1979.
Hundreds of recipes, music, and crafts projects for gifts and decorations for every kind of Jewish celebration.

General

Latner, Helen. *The Book of Modern Jewish Etiquette*. Schocken, 1981.
A compendium of information relating to all aspects of Jewish living.

Samuel, Edith. *Your Jewish Lexicon*. Union of American Hebrew Congregations, 1982.
A clear, concise exploration of basic Hebrew words and concepts.

God

Keeping Posted. Volume XXV, Number 3, December 1979, "Jewish Views of God."

Sonsino, Rifat, and Syme, Daniel B. *Finding God*. Union of American Hebrew Congregations, 1986.
This book presents a variety of Jewish views concerning God.

History

Bamberger, Bernard J. *The Story of Judaism.* Schocken, 1964.
Over 3,000 years of Jewish existence distilled into a single readable volume.

Eban, Abba. *My People: The Story of the Jews.* Random House, 1984.
Written in an elegant style, this book is particularly strong on the modern period.

Eisenberg, Azriel; Goodman, Hannah Grad; and Kass, Alvin. *Eyewitnesses to Jewish History: From 486 B.C.E. to 1967.* Union of American Hebrew Congregations, 1972.
Collection of firsthand reports by people who themselves lived through major events in Jewish history. Some of the events "witnessed" include the revolt of the Maccabees, the Spanish Inquisition, the uprising in the Warsaw Ghetto, and the capture of Eichmann.

Grayzel, Solomon. *A History of the Jews.* New American Library, 1968.
A very reliable one-volume history, geared to the general reader.

Potok, Chaim. *Wanderings.* Fawcett Crest, 1984.
A readable one-volume history, lavishly illustrated.

Roth, Cecil. *A History of the Jews: From Earliest Times through the Six Day War.* Revised edition. Schocken, 1970.
Popular history tracing the social, religious, and cultural development of the Jewish people from the biblical era down to the present.

Sachar, Abram L. *History of the Jews.* Knopf, 1967.
A complete history of thirty centuries of Judaism, in which due emphasis is given to the economic, social, and environmental factors, as well as to religious and philosophical development.

Sachar, Howard M. *The Course of Modern Jewish History.* Dell, 1977.
Comprehensive and scholarly account of the Jews from the French Revolution to the present day. Depicts the social and cultural influences—both Jewish and non-Jewish—that have formed the civilization of Jews throughout the world.

Seltzer, Robert M. *Jewish People, Jewish Thought: The Jewish Experience in History.* Macmillan, 1980.
Comprehensive one-volume overview of the Jewish people's social and political history set against the intellectual, religious, and cultural

currents of the times and places in which Jews lived. An ambitious work, complete with maps, illustrations, and photographs.

Zborowski, Mark, and Herzog, Elizabeth. *Life Is with People: The Culture of the Shtetl.* Schocken, 1962.
   Anthropological study of the world of Eastern European Jewry dealing with, among other things, the Sabbath, *tsedakah,* marriage, and the Jewish home.

Holidays, Festivals, and the Sabbath

Agnon, Shmuel Y. *The Days of Awe.* Schocken, 1965.
   Agnon's classic anthology of Jewish wisdom, skillfully crafted as a literary tone poem on the High Holy Days.

Bearman, Jane. *The Eight Nights: A Chanukah Counting Book.* Union of American Hebrew Congregations, 1979.
   A lively rhyme for each of the eight nights and exquisite full-color graphics present all the delights of *Chanukah*—lighting candles, singing songs, playing *dreidel,* eating *latkes,* and giving and receiving presents. An imaginative activity book for the very young.

Bin-Nun, Judith, and Einhorn, Franne. *Rosh Hashanah: A Holiday Fun-text.* Union of American Hebrew Congregations, 1978.
   A book about *Rosh Hashanah* for young children, encouraging their creative participation.

Cashman, Greer Fay. *Jewish Days and Holidays.* SBS International, 1979.
   A lavishly illustrated book for children, depicting the joy and celebration of the Jewish holidays.

Gaster, Theodor H. *Festivals of the Jewish Year.* William Sloane Assoc., 1953.
   The origins, rituals, customs, and contemporary meaning of the Jewish festivals, fasts, and holy days.

Goodman, Philip, ed. *The Hanukkah Anthology.* The Jewish Publication Society of America, 1976.
   The seven holiday anthologies edited by Philip Goodman are useful guides for meaningful celebration. Each volume contains sections on the history of the holiday and its observance, the representation of the day in art, poetry and prose readings from both the ancient and modern sources, and the music associated with the celebration.

_____. *The Passover Anthology*. The Jewish Publication Society of America, 1961.

_____. *The Purim Anthology*. The Jewish Publication Society of America, 1949.

_____. *The Rosh Hashanah Anthology*. The Jewish Publication Society of America, 1970.

_____. *The Shavuot Anthology*. The Jewish Publication Society of America, 1975.

_____. *The Sukkot and Simhat Torah Anthology*. The Jewish Publication Society of America, 1973.

_____. *The Yom Kippur Anthology*. The Jewish Publication Society of America, 1971.

Heschel, Abraham J. *The Sabbath*. Farrar, Straus and Giroux, 1975.
   The author's magical celebration of the Sabbath and the sanctification of time over space.

Knobel, Peter S., ed. *Gates of the Seasons: A Guide to the Jewish Year*. Central Conference of American Rabbis, 1983.
   This book, written from a Reform perspective, provides background and suggestions for observing all the holidays.

Marcus, Audrey F., and Zwerin, Raymond A. *But This Night Is Different*. Union of American Hebrew Congregations, 1981.
   Beautiful, sensitive portrayal of *Pesach*. For ages six to eight.

_____. *A Purim Album*. Union of American Hebrew Congregations, 1981.
   A charming book about *Purim* for young children. For ages six to eight.

_____. *Shabbat Can Be*. Union of American Hebrew Congregations, 1979.
   The warm feelings and images of *Shabbat* familiar to a small child are evoked in the simple text and lovely illustrations. For ages six to eight.

Millgram, Abraham. *Sabbath: The Day of Delight*. The Jewish Publication Society of America, 1944.
   An anthology of materials about the Sabbath, its observance, art, poetry, music, literature, etc.

Schauss, Hayyim. *The Jewish Festivals: History and Observance*. Schocken, 1973.

Details the colorful story of the Jewish festivals and their development, their origin and background, their rich symbolism, ritual practices, and use of ceremonial objects.

A Shabbat Manual. Central Conference of American Rabbis, 1972.

A practical guide to the observance of *Shabbat,* including home services, *Shabbat* songs, selected readings, and a catalogue of the weekly Torah and *haftarah* portions. A tape of blessings and *Shabbat* songs can be ordered with the manual.

Strassfeld, Michael. *The Jewish Holidays: A Guide and Commentary*. Harper and Row, 1985.

A description of holiday customs and observances, with lively wide-ranging commentaries by modern Jewish thinkers.

Holocaust

Dawidowicz, Lucy S. *The War Against the Jews 1933–1945*. Bantam Books, 1976.

A major study of the Holocaust. Intensively researched, comprehensive, and authoritative.

Dobroszycki, Lucjan, ed. *Chronicle of the Lodz Ghetto*. Yale University Press, 1984.

An eyewitness chronicle of the day-by-day events experienced by Jews in the Lodz Ghetto.

Eliach, Yaffa. *Hasidic Tales of the Holocaust*. Avon, 1982.

A varied collection of tales that stresses spiritual rather than physical resistance to the Nazis.

Frank, Anne. *Anne Frank: The Diary of a Young Girl*. Revised edition. Doubleday, 1967.

The remarkable, timeless diary of a young girl, describing the changes wrought upon eight people hiding from the Nazis for two years during the occupation of Holland.

Friedlander, Albert H., ed. *Out of the Whirlwind: A Reader of Holocaust Literature*. Schocken, 1976.

A thorough and fascinating collection of writings, music, and art about the Holocaust. Includes selections by Elie Wiesel, Anne Frank, Leo Baeck, and Abraham J. Heschel.

Bibliography

Hersey, John. *The Wall*. Modern Library, 1967.

A powerful work of historical fiction written in diary form about life in the Warsaw Ghetto during the Nazi occupation.

Hilberg, Raul. *The Destruction of the European Jews*. Harper and Row, 1979.

A detailed presentation of the events of the Holocaust with particular attention given to the specifics of the Nazis' war against the Jews.

Morse, Arthur D. *While Six Million Died: Chronicle of American Apathy*. Hart, 1975.

The author builds a convincing case of U.S. governmental indifference and national apathy in the face of the Holocaust. A significant and powerful report.

Rabinowitz, Dorothy. *New Lives: Survivors of the Holocaust Living in America*. Avon, 1977.

The survivors themselves tell of individual reactions to liberation, arrival in America, starting new jobs and homes and families, and finding their place in a world that did not understand the nightmare from which they had emerged.

Schwarz-Bart, André. *The Last of the Just*. Translated from the French by Stephen Becker. Bantam Books, 1973.

Memorable novel about the Holocaust, using the theme of the thirty-six just souls through whose merit the world continues to exist.

Shabbetai, K. *As Sheep to the Slaughter? The Myth of Cowardice*. World Association of the Bergen-Belsen Survivors Associations, 1963.

Deals with the misconception that Jews went to their deaths without offering resistance.

Spiritual Resistance: Art from the Concentration Camps, 1940–1945. Union of American Hebrew Congregations, 1981.

The 111 color and black and white reproductions reveal the Holocaust as seen by those who witnessed and suffered the terrors of Nazi extermination efforts.

Wiesel, Elie. *Night*. Avon, 1972.

Powerful, autobiographical account of a young boy's experiences during the Holocaust.

Israel

Chafets, Ze'ev. *Heroes and Hustlers, Hard Hats and Holy Men*. William Morrow and Company, 1986.

A very readable impressionistic sketch, which captures the spirit of contemporary Israel.

Grose, Peter. *Israel in the Mind of America*. Schocken, 1983.

An examination of the development of U.S. government policy toward Israel. The author of this meticulously researched book has worked as a foreign correspondent for the *New York Times* and in the U.S. State Department.

Hertzberg, Arthur, ed. *The Zionist Idea*. Atheneum, 1959.

An extensive collection of essays and readings on Zionist ideology.

O'Brien, Conor Cruise. *The Siege*. Simon and Schuster, 1986.

Israel is a country under siege, and this book, written by an Irish diplomat-journalist-scholar, deals with the international, cultural, political, and diplomatic aspects of that siege.

Oz, Amos. *In the Land of Israel*. Harcourt Brace Jovanovich, 1983.

After the invasion of Lebanon, one of Israel's preeminent authors interviewed a cross section of the Israeli population. This book resulted from those interviews and raises powerful questions about the meaning and future of Israeli life.

Sachar, Howard M. *A History of Israel: From the Rise of Zionism to Our Time*. Knopf, 1979.

Best one-volume history of the modern State of Israel. Meticulously researched and intelligently written.

Jewish Religious Movements

Borowitz, Eugene. *Reform Judaism Today*. Behrman House, 1983.

Written by a leading Reform scholar, this book presents the evolution of the Reform movement and the author's view of its future.

Gordis, Robert. *Understanding Conservative Judaism*. Ktav, 1978.

An introduction to Conservative Judaism by a highly regarded Conservative scholar.

Grunfeld, Isadore. *Judaism Eternal*. Soncino Press, 1956.

This volume presents an Orthodox approach to Judaism.

Kaplan, Mordecai M. *Judaism as a Civilization*. The Jewish Publication Society of America and Reconstructionist Press, 1981.
    The seminal document that led to the establishment of the Reconstructionist movement.

Keeping Posted. Volume XXVI, Number 3, December 1980, "Conservative Judaism."

——————————. Volume XXV, Number 4, January 1980, "Orthodox Judaism."

——————————. Volume XXVII, Number 3, January 1982, "Reconstructionism."

——————————. Volume XXIV, Number 1, September 1978, "What Is Reform?"

Segal, Abraham. *One People*. Union of American Hebrew Congregations, 1982.
    A textbook-workbook dealing with the misconceptions about Judaism's main branches, the differences that separate them, and the similarities that make them one people.

Jewish Thought and Philosophy

Borowitz, Eugene. *Modern Varieties of Jewish Thought: A Presentation and Interpretation*. Behrman House, 1981.
    A thoughtful presentation and analysis of the philosophies of the major thinkers of our time. Includes chapters on Hermann Cohen, Leo Baeck, Mordecai Kaplan, Franz Rosenzweig, Martin Buber, Abraham Heschel, and Joseph D. Soloveitchik.

Cohen, Abraham. *Everyman's Talmud*. Schocken, 1975.
    An explanation of the Talmud's history and makeup is followed by summaries of the major teachings by subject.

Cohen, Arthur A., and Mendes-Flohr, Paul. *Contemporary Jewish Religious Thought*. Scribner's, 1987.
    Contains hundreds of topics of Jewish relevance explained by leading scholars of each field.

Glatzer, Nahum. *The Judaic Tradition*. Behrman House, 1982.
    A collection of more than 200 texts from great Jewish sources of

ancient, medieval, and modern times. Each selection is introduced and has informative notes.

Guttman, Julius. *Philosophies of Judaism: The History of Jewish Philosophy from Biblical Times to Franz Rosenzweig.* Schocken, 1973.
Authoritative history of Jewish philosophy, from biblical times through its period of great vitality in the Middle Ages to the turn of this century.

Heschel, Abraham Joshua. *Between God and Man.* Edited by Fritz A. Rothschild. Free Press/Macmillan, 1965.
Selections from the writings of one of the outstanding Jewish thinkers of the twentieth century.

Holtz, Barry W., ed. *Back to the Sources: Reading the Classic Jewish Texts.* Summit Books, 1984.
This is an outstanding book for someone who wishes to delve into the classic Jewish sources. It not only gives excerpts from Bible, Talmud, Midrash, etc., but also explains how to go about studying these works.

Jacobs, Louis. *The Book of Jewish Belief.* Behrman House, 1984.
A survey of basic Jewish beliefs such as Torah, *mitzvot,* mysticism, ethics, etc.

Steinberg, Milton. *Basic Judaism.* Harcourt, Brace and World, 1947.
An outstanding treatment of the fundamentals of Judaism.

Steinsaltz, Adin. *The Essential Talmud.* Basic Books, 1977.
One of Israel's greatest scholars presents an excellent introduction to the Talmud. This book makes what could be a difficult subject accessible to the general reader.

Weiner, Herbert. *9½ Mystics: The Kabbalah Today.* Macmillan, 1985.
A good basic introduction to Jewish mysticism written in a journalistic style.

Life Cycle
Bial, Morrison D. *Liberal Judaism at Home.* Union of American Hebrew Congregations, 1971.
Easy-to-read guide to Jewish life-cycle events and holidays, giving both traditional and Reform approaches.

_____. *Your Jewish Child*. Union of American Hebrew Congregations, 1978.

A primer to help parents and parents-to-be create a Jewish home that promotes Jewish identity. Topics covered include simple ritual, naming a baby, prayer, and how to tell your children about God, death, and afterlife.

Diamant, Anita. *The New Jewish Wedding*. Summit Books, 1985.

An informative guide, which gives practical suggestions for planning a Jewish wedding.

Feldman, David M. *Marital Relations, Birth Control, and Abortion in Jewish Law*. Schocken, 1974.

Traditional Jewish perspective on marital relations, contraception, and abortion. The author examines these issues through the teachings of the Talmud, codes, commentaries, and rabbinic responsa.

Gittelsohn, Roland B. *Love, Sex, and Marriage: A Jewish View*. Union of American Hebrew Congregations, 1980.

A modern, candid discussion of Jewish sexual ethics. For grade eleven and up.

Goodman, Philip, and Goodman, Hannah, eds. *The Jewish Marriage Anthology*. The Jewish Publication Society of America, 1965.

A volume of ancient and modern sources that depict the unique Jewish understanding of marriage.

Green, Alan S. *Sex, God, and the Sabbath: The Mystery of Jewish Marriage*. Temple Emanu-El, 2200 S. Green Road, Cleveland, Ohio 44121, 1979.

The title is somewhat misleading. This is a beautifully written volume on the meaning of marriage in the Jewish tradition.

Kurshan, Neil. *Raising Your Child to Be a Mensch*. Atheneum Publishers, 1987.

This book deals with the concept of being a *mentsh:* living life in a caring, compassionate, humane way. It conveys means of passing these values on to children.

Lamm, Maurice. *The Jewish Way in Love and Marriage*. Harper and Row, 1980.

A complete treatment of Jewish marriage customs written from an Orthodox perspective.

_____. *The Jewish Way in Death and Mourning*. Jonathan David, 1969.
A complete treatment of Jewish mourning customs written from an Orthodox perspective.

Maslin, Simeon J., ed. *Gates of Mitzvah*. Central Conference of American Rabbis, 1979.
A guide to Jewish observance, throughout the life cycle, from the Reform point of view. Includes sections on birth, childhood, education, marriage, the Jewish home, *tsedakah,* death and mourning, and *kashrut.* Also contains notes and references for further study.

Patz, Naomi, and Perman, Jane. *In the Beginning: The Jewish Baby Book*. Union of American Hebrew Congregations and National Federation of Temple Sisterhoods, 1986.
A beautifully illustrated volume for parents to record important occasions, including Jewish life-cycle events, in their children's lives.

Riemer, Jack, ed. *Jewish Reflections on Death*. Schocken, 1975.
Sensitively chosen collection of essays that portray the historical development and current status of the Jewish way of death.

Routtenberg, Lilly S. *The Jewish Wedding Book*. Schocken, 1967.
A practical guide to planning a Jewish wedding.

Sandmel, Samuel. *When a Jew and Christian Marry*. Fortress Press, 1977.
Addresses and helps clarify the issues relating to mixed marriage.

Schauss, Hayyim. *The Lifetime of a Jew: Throughout the Ages of Jewish History*. Union of American Hebrew Congregations, 1976.
The rites, ceremonies, and folklore that have attended the life of the Jew.

Seltzer, Sanford. *Jews and Non-Jews: Falling in Love*. Union of American Hebrew Congregations, 1976.
An informal guide to interfaith marriage for the couples, their families, and the rabbis who counsel them, from the Reform point of view.

Syme, Daniel B. *The Jewish Home*. Union of American Hebrew Congregations, 1988.
An easy-to-read book describing the holidays and life-cycle events, using a question-and-answer format.

Weilerstein, Sadie Rose. *Our Baby*. Women's League for Conservative Judaism, 1964.

A baby book written especially to mark the milestones and the celebrations of holidays in the life of the Jewish child.

Liturgy

Glatzer, Nahum N., ed. *Language of Faith: A Selection from the Most Expressive Jewish Prayers*. Schocken, 1974.

Prayers from ancient and modern times on such subjects as the Creation, the presence of God, thanksgiving, the cycle of life, Sabbath, and peace.

Hoffman, Lawrence, ed. *Gates of Understanding*. Central Conference of American Rabbis.

Volume One (1977) is a companion volume to *Gates of Prayer*, giving sources for all of the prayers, meditations, and songs. Chapters on the language and origin of prayer, the Reform liturgy, music in Jewish worship, the role of God, and the structure of the prayer book.

Volume Two (1984) is a companion volume to *Gates of Repentance*. It is a lucid explanation of the Reform High Holy Day liturgy.

Millgram, Abraham E. *Jewish Worship*. The Jewish Publication Society of America, 1971.

Surveys the origins, development, and contemporary significance of Jewish liturgy. The author explains all major aspects of Jewish worship and discusses related theological issues as well.

Petuchowski, Jakob J., ed. *Understanding Jewish Prayer*. Ktav, 1972.

The first part deals with the dynamics of Jewish worship from the biblical period through modern times. It discusses such problems as the concept of prayer as "obligation," the place of the Hebrew language in Jewish worship, and the modern challenges to prayer. The second half of the book consists of an anthology of essays on Jewish prayer contributed by outstanding Jewish scholars.

The following are the Conservative movement's *siddur, machzor,* and *haggadah:*

Harlow, Jules, ed. *Siddur Sim Shalom*. The Rabbinical Assembly, 1985.

_____. *Mahzor for Rosh Hashanah and Yom Kippur*. The Rabbinical Assembly, 1972.

Rabinowicz, Rachel Anne, ed. *Passover Haggadah: The Feast of Freedom*. The Rabbinical Assembly, 1982.

The following are the Reconstructionist movement's *siddur, machzor,* and *haggadah:*

Sabbath Prayer Book. The Jewish Reconstructionist Foundation, Inc., 1965.

Kaplan, Mordecai M.; Kohn, Eugene; and Eisenstein, Ira. *High Holyday Prayerbook, Vol. I (Prayers for Rosh Hashanah) and Vol. II (Prayers for Yom Kippur)*. The Jewish Reconstructionist Foundation, Inc., 1948.

Kaplan, Mordecai M.; Kohn, Eugene; Eisenstein, Ira; and Nadelmann, Ludwig, eds. *The New Haggadah*. Revised edition. Behrman House, 1978.

The following are the Reform movement's *siddur, machzor, haggadah,* and home prayer book:

Stern, Chaim, ed. *Gates of Prayer: The New Union Prayerbook*. Central Conference of American Rabbis, 1975.

_____. *Gates of Repentance*. Central Conference of American Rabbis, 1978.

Bronstein, Herbert, ed. *A Passover Haggadah*. Central Conference of American Rabbis, 1974.

Stern, Chaim, ed. *Gates of the House*. Central Conference of American Rabbis, 1976.

Unlike the other movements, Orthodoxy has not published a set of standard prayer books. We have listed an example of an Orthodox *siddur, machzor,* and *haggadah.*

Pool, David De Sola, ed. *The Traditional Prayerbook for Sabbath and Festivals*. Behrman House, 1960.

Scherman, Nosson, ed. *The Complete ArtScroll Machzor*. Mesorah Publications Ltd., 1985.

Riskin, Shlomo. *The Passover Haggadah*. Ktav, 1983.